The body remembers everything

The Mind-Body Connects to the effects and healing of trauma

[Jane. F. Durst]

Copyright © 2025 by [Jane. F. Durst]

The body remembers everything All rights reserved. No part of this publication may be reproduced, distributed, or transmitted in any form or by any means electronic, mechanical, photocopying, recording, or otherwise without the prior written permission of the copyright holder, except in the case of brief quotations used in reviews or scholarly works.

CONTENT

Purpose of This Book.. **9**
    The Science Behind the Body's Memory................ 14
    Historical Perspectives on BodyMemory................ 15
    Defining Trauma... 19
How trauma is stored in the body........................... **20**
    The Impact of Unresolved Trauma on Health......... 23
The Autonomic Nervous System and Memory...... **26**
Fight, Flight, Freeze: Responses to Trauma............ **30**
Techniques for Regulating the Nervous System..... **39**
Listening to Your Body: Symptoms of Repressed Memory... **49**
Pain as a Language: Deciphering Messages from the Body... **55**
Techniques for Developing Body Awareness.......... **63**
The Power of Somatic Experiencing........................ **74**
    Mindful Movement Practices: Yoga, Dance, and More... 83
Case Studies: Transformation Through Movement 95
Psychotherapy and Bodywork: A Holistic Approach. 103
Incorporating Mindfulness and Meditation: Cultivating Presence in Everyday Life..................... **111**
Nutrition and Its Role in Emotional Wellbeing....... **119**
Healing Journeys: Real-Life Experiences.............. **129**

The Process of Reclaiming Memory and Self........138
Lessons Learned from Clients................................148
Journaling as a Healing Tool....................................158
Art and Creative Expression in Processing Trauma... 164
Guided Exercises for Body Awareness..................178
Finding the Right Professionals.............................185
Community and Connection: The Threads That Hold Us Together..188
Reflections on the.. 203
Journey of Healing.. 203
The Future of Mind-Body Practices........................208

Introduction

The Mind-Body Connection

One of the most intricate and intriguing aspect of human experience is the interaction between the mind and the body.For centuries, philosophers, scientists, and healers have tried to understand how Our thoughts, emotions, and mental condition affect our physical health, and vice versa. Today, the concept of a mind-body connection is not just a philosophical idea, but a subject backed by growing scientific evidence and embraced in fields ranging from psychology and medicine to holistic wellness and everyday self-care.

At its core, the mind-body connection suggests that our mental and emotional states can have a direct impact on our physical well-being. When we are stressed, anxious, or emotionally overwhelmed, our bodies often respond with symptoms such as fatigue, muscle tension, headaches, or even chronic illness. On the other hand, positive mental states like happiness, hope, and inner calm can promote better immune function, faster healing, and an overall sense of vitality. It's not magic; it's biology, neuroscience, and psychology working together in intricate harmony.

What makes the mind-body connection especially powerful is its bidirectional nature. Talking care of our body can significantly improve our mental attitude, just as our mental health can influence our physical status.Regular physical activity, for example, has been shown to reduce symptoms of depression and anxiety, while good nutrition and sufficient sleep support clearer thinking and emotional balance. The body and mind do not operate in isolation they are in constant communication through networks of hormones, neurotransmitters, and electrical impulses.

Now more than ever, it is critical to comprehend this connection.In a fast-paced world where stress, distraction, and burnout are common, learning how to align and care for both mind and body can lead to a more balanced, resilient, and fulfilling life. Whether through mindfulness, exercise, therapy, or simply slowing down and listening to our own needs, the tools for nurturing this connection are accessible to everyone.

This introduction sets the stage for a deeper exploration into how thoughts shape biology, how physical health influences emotional well-being, and how an integrated approach to health can help us live more fully and intentionally.

Purpose of This Book.

The body is a living archive, not just a container. Every emotion wes suppress, every trauma we endure, and every moment of joy or sorrow we experience, leaves an imprint somewhere within us. We often think of memory as something stored solely in the brain, but many of our most formative experiences are held in the very tissues of our bodies. This book was born from that understanding.

The purpose of The Body Remembers Everything is to explore how our bodies store and reflect our lived experiences, particularly those we might not even realize have shaped us. While science and psychology have long studied the mind's capacity to remember, we're only beginning to acknowledge the intelligence of the body the way it flinches at a familiar tone, tightens during confrontation, or softens in the presence of safety. These reactions aren't random. Years or perhaps decades of learned survival have led to them. Not everyone who reads this book has a clinical understanding of trauma or body-based therapies. Anyone who has ever asked themself, "Why do I react this way?" should read this. or "Why, even when everything seems fine, do I feel stuck?" Whether you're healing from a specific experience or simply curious about your inner landscape, this book aims to give you language for what your body has been trying to say all along.

It invites readers to consider the body as a partner in healing rather than a passive recipient of stress. Through stories, reflections, and practical insights, the pages ahead offer a space to reconnect with sensations, memories, and ultimately, yourself. The hope is not to relive old pain, but to understand it, move through it, and reclaim the parts of you that might have been lost or silenced.

This book also reminds us that recovery is not a straight path. There is no fixed timeline or universal map. What your body holds, it holds for a reason, and learning to listen to it is a powerful, often transformative, act of self-respect. There is a profound intelligence within you, and this book is meant to help you tune into that wisdom.

Above all, the intention here is to foster compassion for yourself, for the journey you've traveled, and for the resilience you carry. Every step toward awareness is a step toward freedom, and sometimes, the most important breakthroughs come not from changing who we are, but from understanding and honoring what we've been through.

Let this book be a guide, a companion, and a quiet witness to the truth your body has always known: you remember more than you think and that remembrance can lead to healing.

CHAPTER ONE
Understanding Somatic Memory

What Is Somatic Memory?

Somatic memory is the body's way of remembering. Unlike the kind of memory we usually think of facts, dates, names, and events stored in the brain somatic memory is physical. It's the memory that lives in your muscles, nerves, and tissues. This type of memory doesn't rely on words. Instead, it shows up through sensation, posture, reflexes, and sometimes even pain.

Imagine the way your body tenses up when someone raises their voice at you. Or how the scent of a certain perfume can make your stomach twist because it reminds you of something unpleasant, even if you can't quite pinpoint why. Those reactions come from your body remembering something it once went through. That's somatic memory at work.

The Science Behind the Body's Memory

Memory isn't confined to the brain. While we often associate recall and recognition with mental processes, our bodies play a much more active role in storing and responding to memories than we might realize. From the way muscles tighten at the sound of a loud noise, to how the heart races during moments of stress even without a clear reason our bodies are deeply entwined with our experiences. This phenomenon is often referred to as body memory, a concept that explores how physical sensations, movements, and emotional patterns are imprinted into our physiological systems.

What is Body Memory?

The theory that our physical bodies have the capacity to store memories apart from the conscious brain is known as body memory. While this may sound abstract, there's a growing body of research suggesting that emotions, trauma, and learned behaviors can become encoded not just in our minds but in our muscles, nervous system, and even our gut.

Historical Perspectives on BodyMemory

Think about muscle memory for a moment. When you ride a bike, play an instrument, or type on a keyboard, your body seems to "know" what to do without you having to consciously think through each action. These procedural memories are stored in the cerebellum and basal ganglia parts of the brain associated with movement and coordination but they manifest through the body. Over time, these patterns become second nature, enabling fluid and instinctive movement.

However, body memory goes beyond simply practicing skills.It also encompasses emotional experiences particularly those linked to trauma.developments in body psychotherapy and somatic experiencing. By the 1970s and 80s, figures like Alexander Lowen, Peter Levine, and others expanded on these ideas, grounding them in clinical experience and eventually in emerging neuroscience.

Indigenous and Non-Western Traditions

While Western science took centuries to revisit the connection between body and memory, many Indigenous cultures never lost touch with it. In Native American, African, and Aboriginal traditions, healing often involves rituals, dance, and storytelling communal acts that engage both body and spirit. These practices honor the idea that the body carries the legacy of lived experiences, including those of ancestors.

Rituals of shaking, drumming, and movement serve not only as expressions of emotion but also as tools for releasing inherited pain or trauma. Such practices reveal a sophisticated understanding of how memory especially traumatic memory can be embedded in the body and how it can be metabolized through collective, embodied experience.

A Full-Circle Return

Today, as science revalidates what ancient systems always intuited, we're witnessing a re-integration of body and mind in how we understand memory. Research into somatic trauma, neuroplasticity, and epigenetics is giving language and credibility to ideas that were once only found in sacred texts or cultural rituals.

Looking back, it's clear that the history of body memory is less a linear progression and more a pendulum swing between intuition and rationalism, disconnection and integration. What modern medicine is now uncovering through scans, studies, and sensors was, in many ways, already known just spoken in a different tongue, shaped by different hands, and carried through the wisdom of generations who never doubted that the body remembers.

CHAPTER TWO

Trauma and its effect.

Defining Trauma.

Trauma is define as an exceedingly distressing or unpleasant incident that exceeds a person's ability to cope is referred to as trauma. I It can result from a single event (like an accident or natural disaster), repeated experiences (like abuse or neglect), or ongoing stress (like living in a dangerous environment).

There are different types of trauma:

- **Acute trauma** – from a single incident.
- **Chronic trauma** – from repeated and prolonged experiences.
- **Complex trauma** – Exposure to numerous, diverse, and frequently intrusive, interpersonal

traumatic situations can result in complex trauma.

Everybody experiences trauma differently, and it can have an impact on one's physical, mental, and emotional well-being. It frequently takes time, therapy, and support to recover from trauma.

How trauma is stored in the body.

Trauma is often stored in the body as a result of the physiological and psychological responses to stressful or harmful experiences. When an individual experiences trauma, the body's stress response system activates, leading to a release of stress hormones like cortisol and adrenaline. This may lead to changes in breathing patterns, posture, and physical strain.

Over time, unresolved trauma can manifest as chronic pain, muscle tension, or other somatic symptoms, as the body retains the physical memory of the traumatic event. This phenomenon is often referred to as "body memory." Additionally, the nervous system may become hypervigilant or dysregulated, leading to heightened sensitivity and reactions to stressors, even if they are not directly related to the trauma.

Therapeutic approaches such as body-focused therapies, somatic experiencing, and mindfulness can help individuals process and release stored trauma from the body, promoting healing and a return to a state of balance. There are different types of trauma:

Acute trauma – from a single incident.

Chronic trauma – from repeated and prolonged experiences. Trauma is often stored in the body as a result of the physiological and psychological responses to stressful or harmful experiences. When an individual experiences trauma, the body's stress response system activates, leading to a release of stress hormones like cortisol and adrenaline. This may lead to changes in breathing patterns, posture, and physical strain.

Over time, unresolved trauma can manifest as chronic pain, muscle tension, or other somatic symptoms, as the body retains the physical memory of the traumatic event. This phenomenon is often referred to as "body memory." Additionally, the nervous system may become hypervigilant or dysregulated, leading to heightened sensitivity and reactions to stressors, even if they are not directly related to the trauma. Trauma is often stored in the body as a result of the physiological and psychological responses to stressful or harmful experiences. When an individual experiences trauma, the body's stress response system activates, leading to a release of stress hormones like cortisol and adrenaline. This can result in physical tension, altered body posture, and changes in breathing patterns. Therapeutic approaches such as body-focused therapies, somatic experiencing, and mindfulness can help individuals process and release stored trauma from the body, promoting healing and a return to a state of balance.

Exposure to numerous, diverse, and frequently intrusive, interpersonal traumatic situations can result in complex trauma. Everybody experiences trauma differently, and it can have an impact on one's physical, mental, and emotional well-being. It frequently takes time, therapy, and support to recover from trauma.

The Impact of Unresolved Trauma on Health

Unresolved trauma doesn't simply fade with time. Instead, it quietly settles into the body and mind, often showing up in unexpected ways. Many people carry the weight of past experiences without realizing how deeply those events continue to affect their well-being.

Physically, trauma can manifest through chronic pain, fatigue, or even gastrointestinal issues. The body, in its attempt to protect itself, stays in a heightened state of alert sometimes for years. This prolonged stress response can strain the immune system, disrupt sleep, and contribute to conditions like heart disease or high blood pressure.

Mentally and emotionally, unresolved trauma can lead to anxiety, depression, or difficulties with trust and relationships. It may influence how a person sees the world, often creating a sense of fear or hypervigilance.

The brain may continue to operate in survival mode even in secure settings.

What makes trauma especially complex is that it doesn't always come from one major event. Sometimes it's the result of repeated experiences over time such as neglect, emotional abuse, or growing up in a chaotic environment. These patterns shape how the brain develops, especially in children, and can affect decision-making, impulse control, and emotional regulation well into adulthood.

Healing from trauma requires more than simply talking about it. While therapy can be incredibly helpful, so can body-based approaches like yoga, breathwork, or EMDR (Eye Movement Desensitization and Reprocessing). Everybody's rehabilitation path is unique, so it's critical to approach it with compassion and patience.

Ultimately, recognizing the impact of unresolved trauma is a crucial step toward better health. It's not about blaming the past it's about understanding how it shapes the present and choosing to care for ourselves in a deeper, more meaningful way.

CHAPTER THREE

The Role of the Nervous System.

The Autonomic Nervous System and Memory.

When we think about memory, we often picture the brain's role in recalling names, events, or past experiences. However, the autonomic nervous system, or ANS, is another important but frequently disregarded actor. Though it's best known for regulating automatic functions like heartbeat, breathing, and digestion, its influence stretches into how we encode, store, and recall emotional experiences.

The sympathetic and parasympathetic nervous systems are the two primary branches of the autonomic nervous system. These two branches work together to maintain balance in the body, but they also react strongly during emotionally charged events. And it's during these moments of fear, excitement, stress, or calm that memory becomes deeply intertwined with the body's physiological state.

The sympathetic nervous system, also known as the "fight or flight" system, will be discussed first. .commonly known as the "fight or flight" system.When we're faced with a sudden challenge or threat, this system kicks into gear. It increases heart rate, elevates blood pressure, and sharpens focus essentially preparing us to respond quickly. But what's especially interesting is that during these intense moments, our brains are also more likely to lay down strong, lasting memories. That's because stress hormones like adrenaline and cortisol get released, which interact with parts of the brain responsible for memory, such as the amygdala and hippocampus. This is one reason why people often remember traumatic or highly emotional events so vividly, even years later.

On the other hand, the parasympathetic nervous system, known for its "rest and digest" role, becomes active when we're relaxed and at ease. While this system doesn't trigger memory formation in the same way as the sympathetic system, it plays a crucial role in memory consolidation the process by which short-term memories are converted into long-term ones. During restful states, especially sleep, the brain sorts through the day's experiences and stores important information. So, in a way, the calming influence of the parasympathetic system provides the space and conditions for lasting memories to form.

What makes the relationship between the ANS and memory so fascinating is how seamlessly the body and brain cooperate during emotionally significant experiences. We're not just thinking beings we feel our memories. Our heart races when recalling a scary moment. We get goosebumps thinking about a meaningful conversation. That's the autonomic nervous system working hand-in-hand with the brain, reinforcing memories through the body's physical responses.

Even in clinical research, this connection has been explored in studies of PTSD, anxiety, and emotional learning. People who have experienced trauma often have a heightened autonomic response to reminders of that trauma, showing just how deeply memories can be wired into our physical systems.

In summary, while the autonomic nervous system might seem distant from the conscious mind, it plays an essential behind-the-scenes role in shaping how we experience and remember the world. From intense moments that leave a lasting mark to calm periods that allow those impressions to settle, the ANS and memory are constantly in conversation quietly, automatically, and powerfully.

Fight, Flight, Freeze: Responses to Trauma

Trauma has a way of altering how a person interacts with the world often without conscious realization. In moments of intense fear, danger, or threat, the human brain reverts to instinctual reactions that are deeply rooted in evolution. These automatic responses fight, flight, and freeze are not decisions we consciously make. Instead, they are survival mechanisms triggered by the brain's alarm system. Understanding these responses in human terms, through lived emotions and real behaviors, helps illuminate just how deeply trauma can affect the body and mind.

The Fight Response: The Body's Bold Resistance

When the body senses danger and starts the fight response, it gets a boost of energy.Muscles tighten. The jaw may clench.As adrenalin flows through the bloodstream, the heart starts to beat faster.In that moment, the brain sends one clear signal: resist. A person in fight mode might shout, push back, argue aggressively, or throw a punch. By overwhelming the threat, they hope to reclaim control.

This isn't just about physical fights. There are emotional and psychological manifestations of a fight response. A teenager who experienced neglect may lash out when feeling vulnerable, as a defense. An adult who has survived past abuse might become controlling in relationships, trying to avoid any sense of helplessness. Beneath the surface, these behaviors often stem from a desperate need to never feel powerless again.

The Flight Response: Escape at All Costs

Sometimes, standing your ground doesn't feel safe.The brain switches into the flight response at that point.. This is the instinct to run, to get away mentally, emotionally, or physically. A child exposed to constant arguing might grow up craving escape routes: daydreaming in class, running away from home, or later in life, burying themselves in work to avoid personal relationships.

Flight doesn't always mean literal running. It may manifest as avoidance, perfectionism, restlessness, or overthinking.The person is trying to keep moving, because stillness feels like vulnerability. Trauma teaches them that staying in one place emotionally or physically could result in harm.

The Freeze Response: When the World Stops

There are moments when the danger seems too great to resist or run from. In those moments, the brain pulls the emergency brake. This is the freeze response. It's like the mind and body go into a state of suspended animation. Heart rate slows. Movement ceases. Speech may become difficult or impossible. Internally, the person may feel foggy, numb, or disconnected.

This reaction is deeply protective. In nature, animals often freeze to avoid detection. In humans, freeze can be a response to situations where any action feels unsafe. Survivors of trauma may find themselves frozen during arguments, dissociating during stressful events, or unable to speak up in moments that trigger fear. It's not weakness it's a response designed to help the person survive what feels unbearable.

How These Responses Shape Lives

What's crucial to understand is that these reactions are not chosen. They are automatic, encoded by the nervous system. And while they serve a purpose during moments of crisis, they can become problematic when they linger long after the danger has passed. A child who had to freeze to survive a violent household may still freeze in adulthood during minor conflicts. Someone who ran emotionally from a traumatic past may struggle to sit still with difficult feelings or intimacy.

Trauma responses are often misunderstood by others and even by those experiencing them. Someone with a fight response may be labeled "angry" or "difficult." A person who flees might be seen as avoidant or cold. Those who freeze can be misjudged as indifferent. But in reality, these responses tell a deeper story of survival.

Healing Beyond the Response

Recovery begins with recognition. When individuals begin to see these patterns for what they are natural responses to unnatural experiences they can start to reclaim a sense of agency. Therapy, somatic work, mindfulness, and community support can all help soothe the nervous system and rewire these automatic responses.

The goal isn't to erase these instincts. Rather, it's to create space between trigger and reaction, so that a person can respond to life from a place of choice, rather than fear. With compassion, education, and support, those impacted by trauma can move toward healing one breath, one moment, one safe relationship at a time.

without judgment is a transforming technique for the nervous system.Mindfulness increases awareness of internal states and builds the capacity to notice when regulation is needed.Meditation, especially body scans or loving-kindness meditation, can lower cortisol levels, slow the heart rate, and promote greater resilience. Even two to five minutes per day can lead to noticeable changes over time.

1. Creative Expression

Engaging in creative activities such as drawing, writing, knitting, gardening, or playing music can calm the nervous system in profound ways. These acts create a state of "flow," where time falls away and the mind becomes absorbed in the moment.

This focused state fosters regulation because it reduces stress hormones and encourages gentle movement and imagination, both of which nurture the nervous system's need for safety and expression.

2. Nature Immersion

Spending time in natural environments is deeply nourishing for the nervous system. Trees, water, birdsong, and even soil have been shown to reduce stress levels and boost parasympathetic activity. Forest bathing, a Japanese practice known as Shinrin-yoku, is essentially the act of being present in nature. You don't need to hike or camp just sit under a tree, walk barefoot on grass, or stare at the clouds. Nature's pace teaches the nervous system to slow down.

3. Limit Stimulation and Practice Digital Hygiene

Overstimulation from screens, noise, and constant information can keep the nervous system in a chronic state of hyperarousal. Setting boundaries around screen time especially before bed can improve regulation.Simple strategies include using blue-light filters, turning off notifications, and designating "phone-free" zones or hours. Creating sensory breaks throughout the day gives your system room to breathe.

4. Sleep and Rest Cycles

Rest is not a luxury it's a biological necessity. Deep, restorative sleep helps regulate every system in the body, especially the nervous system. Lack of sleep increases reactivity and reduces the ability to self-regulate.Aim to wind down with dim lights, gentle music, and calming activities before bed.Establishing a regular sleep schedule tells the body it's okay to relax and recover.

Techniques for Regulating the Nervous System

Your breath is one of the most basic and powerful tools.The nervous system, responsible for managing stress, focus, and rest, often takes the hit from our chaotic schedules, constant notifications, and never-ending to-do lists. But the good news? With a little education and continuous practice, you can assist your body return to a state of balance.Regulating your nervous system isn't just about avoiding stress it's about building resilience, staying grounded, and improving your overall well-being.

Understanding the Nervous System First

Before diving into techniques, it's important to know the basics.The two neurological systems are the parasympathetic nervous system, sometimes called the "rest and digest" system, and the sympathetic nervous system, sometimes dubbed the "fight or flight" system.When you're stressed, the sympathetic system takes over your heart rate spikes, muscles tense, and your body prepares to react. While that can be helpful in emergencies, staying in this heightened state for too long can cause burnout, anxiety, and physical health issues.

Regulation is about helping the body return to the parasympathetic state after periods of stress, and ideally, spending most of your time in that calm, restorative mode.

1. Breathwork: A Direct Line to Calm

Your breath is one of the most basic yet powerful tools.. The way you breathe sends signals to your brain about how safe or threatened you feel. Shallow, rapid breaths can reinforce anxiety, while slow, deep breaths encourage a sense of safety.

.Try this: Take a four-count breath via your nose, hold it for four, and then slowly release it through your mouth for six.Repeat for a few minutes. This practice, sometimes called "box breathing" or "resonance breathing," helps activate the parasympathetic system and calm the mind.

2. Cold Exposure: Inviting Resilience

Cold showers or splashing cold water on your face may sound uncomfortable, but brief exposure to cold can teach your body how to respond to stress with more ease.It causes a brief sympathetic reaction before a strong transition into the parasympathetic state.

Start small by trying 15 to 30 seconds of cold water at the conclusion of your warm shower. Over time, you may notice improved mood, focus, and stress tolerance.

3. Movement and Exercise: Shaking Off Stress

Physical movement is nature's built-in reset button. It helps release pent-up energy, increases circulation, and encourages the production of feel-good chemicals like endorphins. You don't need an intense workout to feel the benefits even a 10-minute walk can do wonders.

If you're feeling anxious or agitated, try something rhythmic like dancing, jogging, or even bouncing on your toes. .Your nervous system can release tension and regain homeostasis with the aid of these repeating motions.

4. Grounding Techniques: Reconnecting with the Present

Grounding is all about anchoring yourself in the present moment. When the nervous system is dysregulated, it's often because your brain is spiraling into "what if" scenarios or reliving past stress. Grounding pulls you back into what's real and controllable.

Tactile techniques: Touch something with texture run your fingers along a rough surface, hold an ice cube, or rub your hands together.

Sensory groundings: Give the names of five visceral, four tactile, three auditory, two olfactory, and one gustatory items. This exercise shifts attention away from internal chaos and towards external awareness.

5. Mindfulness and Meditation: Training the Brain to Pause

Mindfulness isn't just about sitting cross-legged and thinking about nothing it's the practice of observing your thoughts, feelings, and sensations without judgment. Over time, this builds emotional regulation and makes it easier to ride out stress without getting swept away.

Start with short sessions just five minutes of focused breathing or body scanning. Let your mind wander without scolding it; gently return to the breath each time. With regular practice, your brain starts to create new pathways that support calm and clarity.

6. Vagal Tone Stimulation: Tuning the Nerve of Calm

The vagus nerve plays a huge role in regulating the nervous system. It runs from the brainstem down to the gut and influences digestion, heart rate, and emotional regulation. Improving your vagal tone helps the parasympathetic system engage more efficiently.

How to stimulate it?

Humming or singing loudly

Gargling water vigorously

Laughing deeply

Engaging in deep diaphragmatic breathing

These simple actions create vibrations that activate the vagus nerve and promote a state of calm.

7. Connection: The Healing Power of Relationships

Human beings are wired for connection. Safe, supportive relationships can naturally regulate the nervous system. Think of how a baby is soothed by a caregiver's voice or how a hug can melt stress away that's co-regulation in action.

Spending quality time with loved ones, making eye contact, or simply being present with someone else in a non-judgmental way can help bring your system back into balance.

8. Sleep and Rest: Non-Negotiable Reset

No matter how many techniques you try, they won't work as effectively without enough rest. Your body heals, integrates experiences, and resets when you sleep. Poor sleep increases cortisol (the stress hormone), weakens immunity, and makes emotional regulation harder.

Establish a calming bedtime routine, avoid screens an hour before sleep, and keep your sleep environment cool and dark. Think of rest as an active part of your regulation toolkit not laziness, but recovery.

9. Nutrition: Feeding a Balanced Nervous System

Your gut and brain are deeply connected. In fact, the gut is often called the "second brain." What you eat impacts how you feel and vice versa. Highly processed foods, sugar, and caffeine can disrupt the nervous system, while whole foods rich in healthy fats, proteins, and fiber help stabilize mood and energy.

Include foods that support brain health, like leafy greens, berries, salmon, and fermented foods. Stay hydrated, and notice how your body responds to different meals and snacks.

10. Nature and Sunlight: Nature's Nervous System Tonic

Spending time outside, especially in natural settings, has profound effects on the nervous system. The sun helps regulate circadian rhythms and boosts mood via vitamin

D. Forests and green spaces have been shown to reduce cortisol and blood pressure.

Even just stepping outside for a few minutes, standing barefoot in the grass, or sitting under a tree can help reset your internal rhythm.

The goal of nervous system regulation is to learn how to deal with stress more easily and with less discomfort, not to completely avoid it. These practices aren't magic fixes, but when used consistently, they reshape the way your body and mind respond to the world. Over time, what once triggered panic or exhaustion may become manageable. You become more resilient, more connected to yourself, and more capable of handling whatever comes your way.

Start small. Choose one or two techniques that resonate with you, and slowly build from there. It's never too late to provide the assistance your nervous system requires; it's listening.

CHAPTER FOUR

Recognizing Body Signals.

Listening to Your Body: Symptoms of Repressed Memory

Our bodies are powerful storytellers, often speaking when our conscious minds cannot. Deep within us, certain experiences especially painful or traumatic ones may be tucked away, hidden from our everyday awareness. This phenomenon, often referred to as repressed memory, isn't just a psychological concept; it's a reality that can manifest in subtle, yet impactful, ways throughout the body and mind.

Understanding Repressed Memories

Repressed memories are thoughts, feelings, or recollections that have been unconsciously blocked due to the distress they cause. The mind, in an effort to protect itself from overwhelming pain, may hide these memories. However, repression does not erase the experience it simply buries it. Over time, these buried memories may attempt to surface, not through vivid recollection, but through bodily sensations, emotional shifts, and behavioral changes.

The Body Keeps the Score

Trauma has a unique way of embedding itself into the fabric of our being. As psychiatrist Dr. Bessel van der Kolk aptly describes in his book The Body Keeps the Score, the body holds onto trauma in ways the mind can't always access. The result? A host of symptoms that can seem confusing or unexplainable on the surface, but often point to something deeper trying to be acknowledged.

1. Physical Tension and Unexplained Aches

One of the most telling signs that your body is holding onto a repressed memory is chronic tension particularly in the shoulders, neck, or back. This tightness can persist despite massages, stretches, or even physical therapy. You may also experience phantom aches or persistent fatigue, with no medical diagnosis to explain it. These physical sensations often act as silent reminders of past trauma that your mind has locked away.

2. Emotional Outbursts or Numbness

Some people find themselves overreacting to seemingly minor events, while others feel nothing at all. These represent the two sides of a single coin. Unprocessed emotions tied to repressed memories can erupt suddenly in anger, fear, or sadness. Conversely, you might feel emotionally flat disconnected from joy, love, or even sorrow. This emotional numbing may be a defense mechanism that keeps you safe from the agony that's inside of you.

3. Anxiety Without a Source

It's not unusual for individuals carrying repressed trauma to experience anxiety that doesn't seem to have a clear origin. Panic attacks, restlessness, and chronic worry can all be symptoms. The mind may not recall the trauma, but the body remembers the danger and stays in a state of alert, always anticipating harm, even when you're objectively safe.

4. Trouble with Memory or Concentration

Ironically, while the brain is busy hiding certain memories, it may also struggle to function smoothly in other ways. Difficulty concentrating, frequent forgetfulness, or a feeling of being mentally "foggy" can be signs of a mind that's working overtime to keep certain things hidden. It's as if your mental bandwidth is partially taken up by something you can't quite name.

5. Distorted Sense of Time or Identity

Some people with repressed memories describe feeling disconnected from their own life stories. Time may feel disjointed.certain years might seem like a blur, or entire chunks of one's personal history might feel inaccessible. In extreme cases, individuals might feel like they're watching their life from outside their body, a phenomenon known as dissociation. This can contribute to a fragile or fragmented sense of self.

6. Nightmares and Disturbing Dreams

Dreams often offer a window into the unconscious mind. Individuals dealing with repressed trauma may have vivid, confusing, or frightening dreams. These dreams might not always be literal replays of a traumatic event, but they often carry the same emotional weight fear, helplessness, shame, or confusion. Over time, they can become a cue that something unresolved lies beneath the surface.

7. Triggers Without Explanation

Certain places, smells, sounds, or even phrases may elicit a strong emotional reaction, leaving you confused about the intensity of your response. These triggers often don't make sense logically but they don't have to. The emotional brain recognizes cues that remind it of a past trauma, even if your conscious mind doesn't recall the event.

Listening Without Judgment

Recognizing these symptoms can be unsettling. It's important to approach them with compassion rather than fear or shame. Repressed memories are not a sign of weakness or failure they are evidence of your mind doing its best to protect you when you didn't have the tools to cope.

If you're noticing these signs in yourself, the first step is simply to listen. Start by tuning into your body. Where do you feel tension? What emotions come up throughout the day? Do certain situations make you feel disproportionately anxious or upset?

Mindfulness, journaling, and gentle self-inquiry can help you begin this dialogue with yourself. But often, working with a trained therapist particularly one experienced in trauma and memory work can offer a safe space to explore and process what your body has been holding.

Healing is Not Remembering—It's Reconnecting

While it's natural to want to "recover" memories or seek clarity, healing doesn't always mean recalling every detail. It means learning to feel safe in your own body again. It means creating space for your emotions, learning to trust your intuition, and reestablishing a sense of peace and groundedness.

Your body has likely been trying to get your attention for a long time. Maybe now is the moment to gently lean in, to listen with patience and curiosity, and to let the story unfold not all at once, but step by step, breath by breath.

Pain as a Language: Deciphering Messages from the Body

We often think of pain as something to eliminate a nuisance, a malfunction, an interruption to life. We reach for painkillers, we stretch, we ignore it. But what if pain is not just a problem, but a message? What if, instead of something to silence, pain is something to understand?

Our bodies have no spoken language. They don't use words to express discontent or fear. Instead, they rely on sensations tightness, burning, aching, stabbing. Pain is one of the body's most direct forms of communication. And like any language, it has its own rhythm, vocabulary, and context. Learning to listen to pain, rather than simply shut it down, can unlock a deeper connection with yourself and even illuminate truths you've been avoiding.

The Nature of Pain

Pain can be acute or chronic, physical or emotional, sharp or dull, localized or vague. It's incredibly personal no two people feel pain in exactly the same way. It can signal something simple, like muscle strain, or something complex, like unresolved grief. Pain may begin in the body but often carries an emotional undercurrent, hinting at an internal story waiting to be heard.

Pain is never random. Whether it's a persistent headache, tightness in the chest, or a knot in the stomach, it often reflects more than just physical strain. The body, in many ways, acts as a mirror for the mind and spirit. It absorbs what words cannot express.

When Pain Speaks: Common Messages from the Body

1. **The Weight of Unspoken Emotion**

Have you ever seen how stress gathers in your shoulders or how sadness resides in your throat?Emotions we avoid or suppress don't just disappear they find shelter in the body. Over time, unprocessed feelings like anger, fear, or heartbreak can manifest as physical symptoms.

A clenched jaw may reflect suppressed rage. A heavy chest might point to sorrow you haven't allowed yourself to feel. A stomach that churns with anxiety may be reacting to something in your life that feels unsafe or uncertain. Pain, in these cases, is not just physical—it's emotional energy waiting to be recognized.

2. **Fatigue as a Boundary Cry**

Chronic exhaustion can be the body's way of saying, "I've had enough." Not just physically, but emotionally and mentally. It may be telling you that you're giving too much, pushing too hard, or neglecting your own needs. Fatigue often appears when you've ignored your internal limits for too long.It's your body's cry for repair, not a sign of laziness.

3. Recurring Pain as a Pattern

If the same type of pain keeps returning, it could be more than coincidence. Maybe your lower back always hurts during times of financial stress, or you get migraines when you're trying to please everyone but yourself.Recurrent emotional stressors are frequently associated with recurrent pain.The body remembers even when the intellect tries to forget.

4. Sudden Pain as a Wake-Up Call

Unexpected sharp pain can sometimes act like an alarm bell. It jars you out of routine, forcing attention to a neglected area of your life. Maybe you've been avoiding a difficult decision or staying in a situation that no longer serves you. This kind of pain demands your awareness. It disrupts your rhythm for a reason.

Learning to Interpret the Signals

Deciphering the messages behind pain doesn't mean assuming every ache is psychological. It means considering the whole picture. Where is the pain located? When does it show up? What were you feeling or doing when it began? Are there emotions you've been avoiding?

Here are a few gentle ways to start listening:

Body scanning:Slowly focus on each portion of your body while closing your eyes.. Notice where there's tension, heat, or discomfort. Ask yourself what emotion lives there.

Journaling: Write about your pain as if it were a character.If it could talk, what would it say? What is it attempting to keep you safe from?

Movement: Sometimes movement helps us feel what's hidden. Gentle stretching, yoga, or even dancing can reveal where pain lives and sometimes helps it release.

Mindful presence: Accept the discomfort without attempting to resolve it. Simply take a deep breath. Acknowledgment is frequently the first step toward recovery.

Respecting the Messenger

Pain is not the enemy—it's a messenger.
And like any messenger, its job is to deliver information, not to punish. When we meet pain with curiosity rather than resistance, we can begin to understand what it's pointing toward.

Healing starts with listening.
That listening might reveal that you're living out of alignment with your values, that you're holding onto a relationship or belief that's hurting you, or that you're running on empty trying to meet everyone's expectations

but your own. Pain isn't always about damage it's often about misalignment.

The Body's Wisdom

The body has wisdom our minds don't always grasp. It doesn't lie, and it doesn't forget. It carries the truth of your lived experience your traumas, your joys, your fears. When we ignore its messages, we risk living disconnected, fragmented lives. But when we learn to interpret its language, we become more whole.

So next time pain knocks on your door, consider pausing before you rush to silence it. Ask what it needs. Ask what it's trying to tell you. Beneath the discomfort, there may be a lesson, a truth, or a deep knowing trying to guide you home to yourself.

Techniques for Developing Body Awareness

We frequently lose touch with our bodies in the hustle and bustle of everyday life. We're busy thinking, planning, and pushing forward, yet rarely do we pause to ask, How do I feel physically right now? Body awareness the ability to sense, understand, and connect with the internal landscape of our physical selves is not just a wellness buzzword. It's a vital skill that helps us live more grounded, healthy, and authentic lives.

Developing body awareness is not about achieving some perfect state of mindfulness. It's about learning to listen more closely, to trust what your body is saying, and to respond with care. Whether you're trying to manage stress, heal from trauma, deepen your emotional understanding, or simply become more in tune with your everyday experience, body awareness is the key.

Why Body Awareness Matters

Your body holds an immense amount of wisdom It notices things your mind may overlook. Subtle cues like tension in your chest, butterflies in your stomach, or tightness in your throat can tell you how you're actually feeling long before words catch up.Tuning into these signals helps with emotional regulation, reduces anxiety, improves posture, supports better decision-making, and fosters deeper self-connection.

And perhaps most importantly, when you reconnect with your body, you begin to reclaim parts of yourself that the world might have taught you to ignore.

Below are techniques that can help you begin or deepen the journey of body awareness. These practices don't require special equipment or deep experience—just a willingness to slow down and pay attention.

1. **Body Scan Meditation**

It's simple but powerful.One of the fundamental exercises for cultivating somatic awareness is the body scan.

Find a quiet space, lie down or sit comfortably, and bring your attention slowly through each part of your body, starting from the feet and moving upward. Notice the sensations, temperature, or pressure. Is there tension? Numbness? A surprising emotion?

The important thing is to observe without passing judgment, not to correct or alter anything.Over time, this practice helps you recognize how different emotions and experiences live in different parts of your body.

Why it works:

It cultivates a habit of checking in. The more you notice what your body is saying, the less likely you are to ignore pain, overexert yourself, or suppress your emotional signals.

2. **Breath Awareness**

One of the quickest ways to connect with the body is by breathing.It's always there, always moving, always available.

Start by focusing on your breathing without trying to control it. What part of your body is most affected?Your chest? Belly? Throat? Is it shallow or deep? Fast or slow?

You can deepen the practice by gently guiding your breath into areas that feel tense. For example, breathing into your hips, shoulders, or jaw can help release held tension and increase awareness of those areas.

Why it works:

Breath awareness connects the nervous system with conscious attention. It slows the mind and grounds you into the physical moment, making it easier to tune in.

3. **Movement-Based Practices**

You don't need to be an athlete or a dancer to explore movement. Gentle practices like yoga, tai chi, or even mindful walking can help you become more aware of how your body moves, holds tension, or responds to different emotions.

The goal isn't perfection it's presence. Pay attention to how your body feels as it stretches, bends, or balances.

What movements feel fluid? What feels restricted? What memories or feelings arise with certain postures?

Why it works:

Movement bypasses intellectualization. It brings you directly into the experience of your body and helps release emotions or sensations that words may not reach.

4. **Journaling the Body's Story**

Writing can be a powerful way to deepen body awareness especially when paired with observation.

After a body scan, workout, or emotionally charged moment, try journaling what you felt in your body. Was there tightness in your chest when you spoke up? Did your hands shake before a challenging discussion? What might that sensation be trying to tell you?

These entries can eventually assist you in identifying emotional landscapes, triggers, and patterns associated with bodily sensations.

Why it works:

It creates a bridge between physical sensation and cognitive understanding, helping you connect your emotional world with your body's responses.

5. **Engaging the Senses**

Body awareness isn't limited to internal sensation..Your senses what you see, hear, touch, taste, and smell are also involved. Using your senses with awareness brings you back to the real world.

Try activities like:

Eating slowly and noticing texture, flavor, and aroma

Taking nature walks and observing light, color, and temperature

Listening to music with your eyes closed and feeling it in your body

Using textured objects (stones, fabrics, leaves) and exploring their feel

Why it works:

It helps you reconnect with the richness of the physical world and brings you out of overthinking and into embodied presence.

6. Naming Sensations

When you experience a physical feeling tension, pressure, heat try to name it. Use descriptive words like sharp, dull, buzzing, hollow, prickly, heavy, fluttery. Then go deeper: what emotion might this sensation be linked to?

A tight stomach, for instance, could be a sign of anxiousness. Depression may be indicated by limb heaviness.Learning to name both the physical and emotional components of sensation sharpens your somatic intelligence.

Why it works:

Naming reduces confusion and amplifies self-trust. When you can clearly articulate what you're feeling physically and emotionally, you're less likely to be overwhelmed or reactive.

7. **Loving Touch and Stillness**

Something as simple as placing your hand over your heart or stomach when you're upset can dramatically shift your awareness. This type of self-contact grounds you and reminds your nervous system that you're safe.

Stillness, too, is powerful. Sitting quietly, without distraction, and simply being present with your body however it feels can bring forward awareness that might be drowned out by daily noise.

Why it works:

Touch releases oxytocin and calms the body. Stillness gives space for buried feelings or sensations to rise gently to the surface.

Final Thoughts: Reclaiming the Dialogue

Developing body awareness is not a one-time effort. an ongoing process a conversation that gets deeper the more you engage in it. Your body is not just a vessel; it's your home, your guide, your companion through everything. Learning to understand its language can lead to profound shifts not only in your physical health but in your emotional clarity, your relationships, and your sense of purpose.

Start small. Listen gently. Honor what arises. Over time, your body will begin to trust you again, and you'll find that you don't just live in your body you live with it.

CHAPTER FIVE

Healing Through Movement

The Power of Somatic Experiencing

We live in a world that often encourages us to think our way through pain. When something feels off, we analyze, explain, rationalize. But not everything can be solved in the mind. Sometimes, healing begins in the body.

Somatic Experiencing (SE) is a gentle yet profoundly transformative approach to trauma healing. Unlike traditional talk therapy, it doesn't require detailed retelling of traumatic events. Instead, it invites you to return to the language of the body—the language of sensation, instinct, and rhythm. At its core, somatic experiencing is about restoring the body's natural capacity to regulate itself, to feel safe, and to move forward without carrying the weight of the past.

What Is Somatic Experiencing?

Developed by Dr. Peter A. Somatic Experiencing, developed by Levine over a number of decades, is based on the notion that trauma is a physiological experience as well as a psychological one. Our nervous system might get trapped in a fight-or-flight or freeze response when faced with something overpowering or terrifying. That "stuckness" can linger for years, manifesting as anxiety, chronic pain, dissociation, or emotional numbness.

SE works by helping individuals safely reconnect with the physical sensations linked to trauma, allowing the nervous system to complete the interrupted survival responses and return to regulation. It doesn't rush or force anything .Rather, it respects the body's cues, knowledge, and pace.

Why the Body Holds the Key

Trauma doesn't only live in memories. It resides in the tension in your shoulders, the shallowness of your breath, the knot in your stomach when someone raises their voice. Even if your mind has moved on, your body might still be reliving the moment it froze, fled, or fought to survive.

What SE does so effectively is bypass the logical brain and go straight to the source the body's felt experience. By working with bodily sensations (known as interoception), you can begin to unwind patterns that traditional therapy may not fully reach.

It's not about remembering the story. It's about completing the response that never got a chance to finish.

How Somatic Experiencing Works

Somatic Experiencing isn't a one-size-fits-all technique. It's more of a fluid framework, guided by trained practitioners who listen closely to both your words and your body's cues. Here's how a session often unfolds:

1. Establishing Safety

The process starts with creating a sense of safety and grounding. SE doesn't push you into intense emotional states. Instead, it helps you find stability first resources in your body, your environment, and your life that you can return to at any time.

2. Tracking Sensation

The practitioner will gently guide you to notice physical sensations in the body. This may seem straightforward, but it has tremendous power. You may notice a flutter in your stomach, a constriction in your chest, or warmth in your hands. These subtle cues are how the body speaks.

3. **Titration**

Rather than diving into overwhelming emotions, SE uses titration exploring trauma in small, digestible doses. You might notice a feeling of unease, then shift your attention to a neutral or positive sensation, like the support of the chair beneath you. This oscillation helps build capacity without retraumatizing.

4. **Pendulation**

This technique involves gently moving between states of discomfort and comfort.It mimics the natural cycle of contraction and release in the body.Over time, this back-and-forth helps the nervous system learn that it's safe to feel and that distress doesn't have to be permanent.

5. **Completion**

As the nervous system releases its held energy, you may feel spontaneous movements, emotions, or shifts. This could look like trembling, crying, or even laughter. These aren't symptoms of something wrong they're signs that the body is discharging what it's been carrying.

What Somatic Experiencing Can Help With

SE has demonstrated significant progress in resolving a variety of problems, such as:

Post-traumatic stress

Anxiety and panic

Chronic pain or tension

Dissociation or feeling "numb"

Emotional overwhelm

Sleep disturbances

Feelings of helplessness or disconnection

It's especially helpful for those who feel stuck, who've tried talking about their trauma but haven't felt much relief. Sometimes, words just aren't enough—and that's okay. The body remembers what the mind can't express.

Somatic Healing is Slow, But Deep

There's something radical about choosing slowness in a culture obsessed with quick fixes. SE isn't about instant results or dramatic breakthroughs. It's a practice of gently returning to yourself, moment by moment.

This slow approach allows for lasting change. As you become more attuned to your inner world, you learn to respond to life from a place of presence, not reactivity. You begin to recognize the early signs of dysregulation and instead of spiraling, you can pause, ground, and return to center.

Learning to Trust the Body Again

For many people, trauma erodes the trust they have in their own body. You may feel betrayed by your physical responses, or disconnected from your instincts. SE offers a path back. It teaches that your body was never the enemy.It actually took every precaution to keep you safe.The shaking, the freezing, the shutting down—these were not failures. They were survival strategies.

Somatic Experiencing helps rewrite that story. It helps you learn to trust your signals again, to feel safe in your own skin, and to reclaim the parts of yourself that trauma forced into hiding.

You Don't Need to Remember to Heal

One of the most powerful truths in somatic work is this: You don't need to remember everything to release it. You don't have to relive every moment of the trauma. Your body knows how to heal sometimes better than your mind does.

What SE offers is not a retelling, but a re-patterning. A chance to complete what was interrupted. A chance to come home to yourself.

Final Thought: The Wisdom Within

In a culture that often disconnects us from our bodies, Somatic Experiencing is a quiet revolution. It reminds us that healing isn't always about thinking harder or pushing through. Sometimes, it's about softening. About listening. About trusting that within us lies a map one written in sensation, in instinct, in breath that knows exactly how to lead us back to safety.

Whether you're just beginning your healing journey or have traveled a long road already, Somatic Experiencing offers a space where your body's voice is not only heard but honored.

Mindful Movement Practices: Yoga, Dance, and More

In a world that constantly asks us to do more, move faster, and be better, it's easy to forget that movement isn't just about reaching goals or burning calories. It's also about coming home to yourself. Mindful movement practices offer a radically different way of experiencing the body not as something to control, but as something to listen to and collaborate with.

Whether through the quiet strength of yoga, the expressive freedom of dance, or the grounded flow of walking meditation, mindful movement invites us to slow down and reconnect with breath, with rhythm, and with the deeper wisdom that lives in our bodies.

What is Mindful Movement?

At its essence, mindful movement means moving your body while being fully present. That means tuning into sensations, staying connected to your breath, and allowing awareness to guide your actions. It's not about performing or perfecting it's about feeling.

Unlike traditional exercise, which can often become mechanical or goal-driven, mindful movement brings attention to the how and why of movement. It's a practice of noticing without judgment how the body wants to move, what it needs, and where it might be holding tension or emotion.

Why It Matters

So many of us live from the neck up. Our days are spent thinking, planning, worrying often without checking in with what our bodies are experiencing. Mindful movement creates space for that connection. It's a way to:

Release physical and emotional tension

Regulate the nervous system

Cultivate inner peace

Explore identity and expression

Reclaim joy in the body

Each mindful movement practice offers its own doorway into this experience. Let's examine a few of the strongest.

Yoga: Union Through Awareness

Yoga is perhaps the most well-known form of mindful movement, but its true power lies far beyond flexibility or posture. At its core, yoga is about union bringing together the body, mind, and spirit through breath, movement, and intention.

From slow, meditative styles like Hatha and Yin to more dynamic flows like Vinyasa and Ashtanga, yoga offers something for every body and every mood. What makes it mindful is the attention to detail: feeling your feet grounded, noticing the expansion of your lungs, sensing where your body resists and where it opens.

Yoga eventually transforms from a physical activity into a method of introspection. A conversation between breath and body. A mirror that reflects your life's journey.

Key Benefits:

Improves flexibility and strength

Calms the mind through breath

Builds resilience and self-awareness

Supports emotional processing through physical release.

Dance: Movement as Expression

Dance is one of the most primal and liberating forms of human expression. Before we had language, we had rhythm. And when done mindfully, dance becomes not just performance, but presence.

This isn't about choreography or technique. It's about how the body wants to move. What does grief feel like when you let your arms carry it? What does joy do to your spine? In mindful dance, the body becomes both the storyteller and the story.

Practices like ecstatic dance, 5Rhythms, and conscious movement encourage unstructured, intuitive motion. There are no right steps. Just the rhythm of your heartbeat, the pulse of the music, and the honesty of your body.

Key Benefits:

Encourages emotional release and creativity.

Cultivates body confidence and freedom.

Reduces stress through embodied rhythm.

Fosters community and connection when done in groups.

Walking Meditation: Movement in Stillness

Sometimes, mindfulness is best cultivated through the simplest actions. Walking meditation practiced in many spiritual traditions invites you to turn something ordinary into something sacred.

In this practice, each step is deliberate. You might walk slowly, barefoot, or in silence, noticing the sensations in your soles, the rhythm of your gait, the feel of the air on your skin. Breathing in… step. Breathing out… step. Being with the flow is more important than where you're heading.

This can be a deeply grounding practice for those who struggle with seated meditation or who feel disconnected from their bodies.

Key Benefits:

Encourages presence in daily life

Connects body with nature or surroundings

Eases anxiety through rhythmic movement

Can be done anywhere, without special equipment

Qi Gong and Tai Chi: The Flow of Energy

Rooted in ancient Chinese medicine and martial arts, Qi Gong and Tai Chi are slow, intentional movement practices that harmonize breath, posture, and energy (or "qi").

These practices are meditative in nature, often described as "moving meditation." Every motion is intentional, purposeful. You move like water, letting energy flow through your joints, limbs, and spine. The slowness is the power inviting you to feel more, not less.

Key Benefits:

Enhances balance and coordination

Reduces tension and supports joint health

Strengthens the connection between body and energy systems

Encourages internal quiet and focus

Somatic Movement: Listening to the Body's Voice

Somatic movement is a broad term that refers to practices designed to help you feel more than you do. Rather than stretching or strengthening muscles, you explore movement as a way to unwind patterns of holding, tension, and trauma.

It's deeply intuitive. You might follow the impulse of a shoulder shrug, the curl of a spine, or the shake of a limb. It's not about form it's about sensation. These movements often emerge spontaneously, guided not by the mind but by the body's need to express, discharge, or integrate.

Practices like Feldenkrais, Body-Mind Centering, and somatic yoga fall into this category.

Key Benefits:

Unwinds chronic tension patterns

Reconnects you with inner emotional states

Encourages natural, unforced movement

Supports trauma healing and self-awareness

Putting It Into Practice

You don't need a yoga mat or a studio to begin. Mindful movement can happen in your kitchen, your backyard, or even at your desk. Try this:

Stand up.

Close your eyes.

Take a slow breath.

Gently move your arms in any way that feels natural.

Notice how your body responds where it wants to go, what it wants to do.

That's it. You've just practiced mindful movement.

The key is curiosity. There is no wrong way to move, only unconscious ways. The moment you bring awareness to your motion, it becomes meaningful.

Final Thought: Your Body Already Knows

Mindful movement isn't about becoming more flexible, graceful, or strong. It's about becoming more honest. It's about remembering that your body is not a machine to push but a companion to understand. A message an invitation to feel, to listen, to come back is conveyed by every shudder, stretch, sway, and silence.

Whether you're bending into a yoga pose, dancing in your living room, or walking through the woods with your eyes open to the present moment, mindful movement is a practice of remembering: I am here. I am whole. I am home in my body.

Case Studies: Transformation Through Movement

Movement has always been at the heart of human expression our earliest form of communication, a means of survival, and a gateway to personal transformation. Across different settings whether in clinical therapy, athletic performance, education, or daily life movement has the power to reshape not just bodies, but identities, emotions, and entire lives. In this section, we explore real-world stories that showcase the deeply transformative potential of movement. These case studies, drawn from various contexts, reveal how intentional physical engagement can lead to lasting change.

Case Study 1: Rediscovering the Body After Trauma – Mia's Story

Mia, a 34-year-old graphic designer, had spent years grappling with the lingering effects of childhood trauma. Although successful in her career, she often felt detached from her own body. Traditional talk therapy helped to an extent, but a turning point came when her therapist suggested incorporating somatic movement into her healing process.

Through a trauma-informed dance therapy program, Mia began engaging in slow, guided movement sessions. The sessions didn't focus on choreography or perfection; instead, they encouraged her to explore sensations, tension, and breath. Over time, she started to feel more present in her body able to identify stress before it overwhelmed her and, most importantly, able to feel safe in her own skin again.

Mia later described her journey not as a dramatic change, but as a quiet unfolding a series of moments where movement gave her access to emotional layers that words alone could never reach.

Case Study 2: Healing Through Athletic Reconnection – Jason's Story

After a serious car accident left Jason with a fractured pelvis and months of limited mobility, doctors warned him that his days of long-distance running were likely over. A former marathoner, Jason's sense of identity took a hit. Recovery was slow, and depression began to settle in.

However, under the care of a physical therapist with a background in movement science and psychology, Jason began a tailored program that blended rehabilitation exercises with elements of mindfulness-based movement. Rather than pushing to "get back" to where he was, Jason was encouraged to explore what his body could do now.

Eventually, he transitioned to low-impact sports like swimming and cycling. Though he never ran another marathon, Jason rediscovered his athletic spirit. The reframe wasn't about reclaiming lost abilities but embracing a new relationship with his body one that honored resilience and adaptability over performance.

Case Study 3: From Classroom Struggles to Confidence – Lila's Story

Lila, a bright 10-year-old with ADHD, struggled with focus and self-regulation in the classroom. Her teachers noticed she was often restless and easily frustrated, but traditional behavioral interventions had limited success.

Her parents enrolled her in a movement-based learning program that incorporated elements of yoga, rhythmic games, and balance activities. Within weeks, they noticed changes. Lila started sleeping better, her emotional outbursts lessened, and she became more engaged in class activities.

What made the biggest difference was that Lila began to see herself differently. Movement gave her an outlet a way to channel her energy constructively. By connecting her brain and body through playful, intentional action,

Lila not only improved academically but also grew more confident and self-aware.

Case Study 4: Reclaiming Identity Through Dance – Elias's Story

At 58, Elias retired early from a high-stress corporate job after a health scare. With time on his hands and a sense of aimlessness, he joined a local adult dance class on a whim—something he hadn't done since his college years.

What started as a casual hobby quickly became a source of deep personal joy. In dancing, Elias discovered a renewed connection to himself a part that had been buried under decades of professional obligations. The group dynamic, the music, and the freedom of movement reawakened a creative spark.

Elias described the experience as "remembering who I was before the world told me who to be." The transformation wasn't just physical; it was spiritual, emotional, and deeply affirming.

Case Study 5: Movement as a Bridge for Connection – Noor and Her Grandfather

Noor, a 16-year-old aspiring choreographer, began recording short dance videos to share on social media. During one visit, her grandfather a quiet man in his seventies who rarely spoke about his past watched curiously and mentioned he used to dance as a young man in his village.

Curious, Noor invited him to show her some moves. That simple exchange sparked an intergenerational bond that reshaped their relationship. They began dancing together weekly, blending traditional folk steps with Noor's contemporary flair. Through movement, they found a common language one that didn't require words but spoke volumes.

Their story illustrates how movement transcends generational divides, becoming a powerful tool for connection, healing, and shared joy.

Final Thoughts

Each of these stories highlights a unique journey, yet they all share a common thread: movement as transformation. Whether it's reclaiming agency after trauma, rediscovering joy, connecting across generations, or simply becoming more attuned to the body's wisdom, these case studies demonstrate the profound power of physical experience in shaping our inner lives.

Movement isn't just about fitness or aesthetics it's about returning to ourselves. It invites us to listen, to feel, and to evolve. And in that evolution, we often find the healing and meaning we didn't know we were searching.

CHAPTER SIX

Integrative Approaches to Healing

Psychotherapy and Bodywork: A Holistic Approach

In recent years, there has been a growing recognition that healing isn't confined to the mind alone. While traditional psychotherapy has long focused on talk-based methods to explore thoughts, emotions, and behaviors, a new wave of practitioners and clients alike are embracing a more integrated model one that includes the body as an essential part of the therapeutic process. This emerging paradigm, often referred to as a holistic approach, combines psychotherapy and bodywork to address not just symptoms, but the entire person.

Rethinking the Mind-Body Divide

For centuries, Western medicine and psychology largely treated the mind and body as separate entities. Descartes' famous proposition "I think, therefore I am" cemented a dualistic view that persisted through the development of modern mental health care. While advances in psychotherapy have undoubtedly transformed lives, this split has also left gaps especially for individuals whose emotional distress is deeply rooted in somatic experience.

Trauma, anxiety, depression, grief, and even chronic stress often manifest physically, sometimes without clear verbal narratives. Clients might come into therapy reporting tension in the shoulders, a perpetual sense of tightness in the chest, or unexplained fatigue. These aren't just side effects they're messages from the body. A holistic approach listens to them.

The Synergy Between Psychotherapy and Bodywork

When psychotherapy is paired with body-centered modalities such as somatic experiencing, breathwork, craniosacral therapy, or massage the results can be profound. Rather than relying solely on cognitive insight, this approach supports individuals in feeling their way through healing.

Consider a client processing grief. Talk therapy might help them name their loss, explore memories, and confront the emotional void left behind. But bodywork can take them into deeper terrain: the knot in the stomach that surfaces when they recall a loved one, the breath that catches during difficult recollections, or the sense of collapse in posture mirroring emotional surrender. These embodied sensations often speak louder than words.

Psychotherapists who integrate body awareness into their practice encourage clients to track internal sensations known in somatic therapy as interoception. Doing so fosters emotional regulation, enhances resilience, and provides a sense of agency in the healing journey.

The Body as an Archive

One of the most compelling arguments for a holistic approach is the idea that the body holds memory. Not just the brain, but the tissues, muscles, and nervous system carry imprints of past experiences. This is particularly valid in trauma situations. A person may have limited conscious memory of a traumatic event, but their body might respond to triggers loud noises, touch, or specific environments with intense reactions.

By incorporating bodywork, therapists can help clients gently access these embodied memories, without forcing them to relive the trauma verbally. Techniques like grounding, guided movement, or therapeutic touch can help discharge trapped energy and create space for integration.

This doesn't mean replacing traditional therapy but enhancing it. The goal is not to bypass the mind, but to bring the body into dialogue with it.

Real-World Applications and Success Stories

In clinical settings, this integrated method has proven especially helpful for clients dealing with complex PTSD, developmental trauma, eating disorders, and chronic anxiety. For example, a woman who has struggled with panic attacks might find that talk therapy alone provides insight but not relief. Adding breathwork and gentle somatic exercises into her sessions could help retrain her nervous system, offering a felt sense of safety she's never experienced before.

Athletes recovering from injury, survivors of abuse, veterans with PTSD, and even corporate professionals dealing with burnout have all found solace in combining cognitive and physical healing. In schools and community programs, body-centered practices like yoga and expressive movement are being introduced alongside counseling services, providing children and teens with tools to manage emotions and develop self-awareness.

Therapist as Witness, Not Fixer

.One of the most important things to take away from real healing experiences is that there is no one-size-fits-all approach.What is appropriate for one person could not be for another.Healing might be systematic or chaotic, calm or loud. Journaling, bodywork, therapy, medication, artistic expression, or all of the above could be part of it. However, commitment is the one element that unites all of these tales. a commitment to the procedure over perfection. to support oneself through challenging times. especially on the challenging days.

A Path Toward Wholeness

Healing is not linear. It often involves revisiting old wounds, unlearning defenses, and navigating uncertain terrain. But when the body is welcomed into the process, something shifts. Therapy becomes more than a conversation it becomes a living, breathing, embodied experience.

A holistic approach acknowledges that we are not just minds talking in chairs, but living organisms shaped by sensation, experience, and movement. It invites the full spectrum of human expression tears, laughter, shaking, stillness, and everything in between. In doing so, it offers a path not just to mental wellness, but to wholeness.p

Incorporating Mindfulness and Meditation: Cultivating Presence in Everyday Life

In an age defined by speed, distraction, and constant digital stimulation, the art of being present has become both rare and revolutionary. Amid the noise of daily obligations and the relentless push to do more, mindfulness and meditation offer a radical counterbalance. They ask us to stop, take a deep breath, and live in the present.Far from being abstract or esoteric, these practices are deeply human, accessible, and increasingly supported by science and experience alike.

Understanding the Essence of Mindfulness.

Mindfulness, at its core, is the simple act of paying attention intentionally, without judgment, to what is happening in the present moment. It doesn't ask us to fix anything or to stop thinking. It just asks us to notice. This could mean observing the breath as it moves in and out, feeling the texture of the air on the skin, or recognizing a surge of frustration without immediately reacting to it.

Although rooted in ancient contemplative traditions, particularly within Buddhism, mindfulness has transcended religious boundaries. Today, it is embraced in therapeutic settings, classrooms, boardrooms, and households across the globe. Why? Because it works. Even a few minutes of mindful awareness can shift our physiology, calm our thoughts, and bring us back to ourselves.

The Role of Meditation in Deepening Awareness

While mindfulness is a quality of attention that can be woven into any moment, meditation is often the structured practice through which we cultivate it. Meditation offers a dedicated space for turning inward free from the usual swirl of demands. It's where we learn to observe our internal landscape without becoming entangled in it.

There are many styles of meditation concentration-based, loving-kindness, body scans, breath awareness, and more. Each approach offers its own entry point, but they share a common purpose: to foster clarity, equanimity, and connection.

Some people imagine meditation as the absence of thought, but that's a myth. The mind will wander that's what it does. The point isn't to stop thinking, but to recognize when attention drifts and gently guide it back.

Each return is like a bicep curl for the brain a strengthening of focus, patience, and presence.

Everyday Integration: More Than Sitting on a Cushion

One of the most empowering aspects of mindfulness is its portability. You don't need a mountaintop, incense, or hours of free time. You need only intention. You can practice mindfulness while brushing your teeth, listening to someone speak, eating lunch, or walking down the street.

It might look like pausing before responding to an email, noticing tension in the body before a meeting, or taking three conscious breaths while waiting in line. Over time, these micro-moments accumulate, rewiring the nervous system toward greater calm and awareness.

Many people start with a formal practice perhaps ten minutes each morning in silence and gradually allow that presence to seep into their daily routine. The goal isn't perfection; it's consistency. One missed day doesn't undo the benefits. What matters is the willingness to return, again and again.

Scientific Backing and Measurable Benefits

Neuroscience has begun to catch up with what practitioners have long known: mindfulness and meditation change the brain. Studies using functional MRI scans show that regular practice can increase gray matter density in areas linked to learning, memory, and emotion regulation, while decreasing activity in the amygdala the region of the brain associated with anxiety and stress.

Psychologically, mindfulness is associated with reduced anxiety, improved attention span, better emotional regulation, and increased compassion for self and others. It's being used to treat conditions ranging from depression and PTSD to chronic pain and insomnia. Even in high-performance environments such as elite sports, executive leadership, and the military mindfulness is proving to be a game-changer.

Beyond the statistics, though, there is a subtly meaningful quality to just being there. The ability to truly experience one's own life without numbing, rushing, or avoiding is its own kind of healing.

Challenges and Misconceptions

Despite its many benefits, integrating mindfulness and meditation isn't always smooth. Beginners often report frustration: "My mind won't stop racing," "I'm not doing it right," or "I don't have time." These are valid concerns, but they stem from common misconceptions.

In actuality, mindfulness isn't about reaching a specific condition. It's about showing up, just as you are. It's okay to feel restless, distracted, or even bored. Rather of being barriers to the practice, those experiences are a part of it.

Another challenge is the expectation of instant results. Like any meaningful change building muscle, learning a language, nurturing a relationship this work takes time. The rewards are often subtle at first: a pause before reacting in anger, a deeper breath during stress, a moment of quiet joy on an ordinary day.

Mindfulness as a Way of Life

Eventually, for many people, mindfulness becomes less of a practice and more of a perspective. It influences their speech patterns, parenting styles, leadership styles, and self-care practices.It fosters a way of relating to life with curiosity instead of reactivity, with gentleness rather than judgment.

This isn't about checking out from the world. In fact, it's quite the opposite. Being mindful encourages us to interact more fully with the present, with others, and with ourselves. It helps us see clearly, choose wisely, and live with intention.

In a culture that often values doing over being, mindfulness and meditation remind us that being is enough. That silence can speak volumes. Meaning, healing, and connection all rest on that presence.

Nutrition and Its Role in Emotional Wellbeing

The adage, "you are what you eat," is often used, but what if it also applied to our mental and physical health? While nutrition has traditionally been seen as the domain of physical fitness and disease prevention, an expanding body of research and clinical observation points to a more holistic truth: what we consume directly affects how we feel not just in the body, but in the mind and spirit as well.

In recent years, the link between food and emotional wellbeing has moved beyond wellness trends into serious scientific inquiry. What we now understand is that nutrition is not just fuel for the body; it's information. The nutrients we absorb influence brain chemistry, hormone regulation, and the gut microbiome all of which play crucial roles in emotional regulation and mental clarity.

The Gut-Brain Connection: More Than a Metaphor

One of the most fascinating developments in modern health science is the discovery of the gut-brain axis a two-way communication pathway between the gastrointestinal system and the brain. The gut, often referred to as the "second brain," is lined with millions of neurons and is responsible for producing over 90% of the body's serotonin, a key neurotransmitter associated with mood stability and happiness.

The gut communicates with the brain in a good way when it is working at its best.However, an imbalanced gut due to poor diet, stress, or antibiotic overuse can contribute to anxiety, depression, irritability, and fatigue.

This makes gut health foundational to emotional wellbeing.Clearer thinking, emotional balance, and increased stress resilience are all supported by a healthy gut flora, which can be fostered by a diet high in fiber, fermented foods, and prebiotics.

Blood Sugar and Mood Swings: The Energy Rollercoaster

We've all experienced it: the sharp dip in energy and mood after a sugary snack or carb-heavy meal. What many don't realize is that unstable blood sugar levels don't just affect physical energy they directly influence emotional states.

When blood sugar spikes quickly due to refined sugars or processed foods, the body compensates with a surge of insulin. This is often followed by a rapid drop, leading to symptoms like irritability, shakiness, fatigue, and brain fog. For some, this rollercoaster happens multiple times a day, creating a background hum of mood swings and mental fatigue.

Balancing meals with protein, healthy fats, and complex carbohydrates helps regulate blood sugar levels and provides sustained energy. The result? A more even emotional keel, fewer crashes, and better concentration.

Key Nutrients for Mental and Emotional Health

Certain nutrients play a more direct role in supporting emotional wellbeing. These include:

Omega-3 Fatty Acids: Found in walnuts, flaxseeds, and fatty fish, omega-3 fatty acids are vital for the growth and operation of the brain.

B Vitamins: Particularly B6, B9 (folate), and B12, these vitamins are critical for neurotransmitter production and nerve function. Deficiencies can lead to fatigue, irritability, and even cognitive decline.

Magnesium: Often referred to as "nature's relaxant," magnesium promotes restful sleep, eases stress, and can lessen the signs of anxiety and melancholy.

Zinc: This trace mineral helps maintain a strong immune system and controls mood. It's found in pumpkin seeds, chickpeas, and red meat.

Iron: Fatigue and a depressed mood can be caused by low iron levels, particularly in women. Incorporating iron-rich foods or supplements when needed can dramatically impact energy and emotional stability.

The building components of neurotransmitters are amino acids. Protein-rich foods like eggs, legumes, and lean meats help the brain produce dopamine, serotonin, and other mood-regulating chemicals.

Emotional Eating: When Food Becomes a Coping Tool

It's impossible to talk about nutrition and emotional wellbeing without acknowledging the complex relationship many people have with food. For many, eating is not just about sustenance it's about comfort, distraction, or even punishment. Emotional eating can become a reflexive way to cope with stress, boredom, loneliness, or grief.

While there's no shame in turning to food for comfort occasionally, consistent patterns of emotional eating can create a cycle of guilt, shame, and physical imbalance. Learning to identify emotional hunger versus physical hunger, and finding alternative tools for self-soothing like journaling, walking, or connecting with others can help restore a more conscious relationship with food.

Mindful Eating: Nourishing the Body and the Mind

Eating mindfully involves more than just what's on the plate.It's about how we eat. When we slow down, pay attention to flavors, textures, and internal signals, we begin to shift our relationship with food from transactional to intimate.

Eating in a calm environment, chewing thoroughly, pausing between bites, and listening to the body's cues can not only improve digestion but also enhance satisfaction. Over time, this presence at mealtime spills over into other areas of life, fostering greater self-awareness and emotional regulation.

Cultural and Social Influences on Nutritional Health

Food is deeply personal and cultural. What nourishes one person might feel foreign or inaccessible to another. Emotional wellbeing around food also involves respecting personal traditions, preferences, and values.

However, modern society often makes balanced nutrition more difficult than it needs to be. Fast food, conflicting dietary advice, time constraints, and food insecurity all present real challenges. Improving emotional wellbeing through nutrition must also consider accessibility and sustainability not just for individuals, but for communities.

A Holistic Perspective on Food and Feelings

Emotional wellbeing is influenced by many factors genetics, environment, relationships, stress, and more. But nutrition is a foundational pillar, one that is often overlooked in favor of more obvious interventions. How we sleep, think, react to stress, and interact with the outside world are all influenced by the food we consume.

While no single food will eliminate depression or anxiety, nourishing the body with real, whole foods can provide the foundation for deeper healing. In combination with other forms of care therapy, movement, community good nutrition becomes a quiet but powerful ally in the journey toward emotional health.

CHAPTER SEVEN

Case Studies and Personal Stories

Healing Journeys: Real-Life Experiences

Healing is rarely a straight path. It curves, it pauses, it sometimes retraces its own steps. While medicine, therapy, and supportive systems play critical roles, there's something deeply personal about the process of healing something that can't be measured in clinical terms or explained by textbooks. Fundamentally, healing is a human experience. It unfolds differently for each individual, shaped by past wounds, inner resilience, and the people and choices that surround us. Experiences from everyday life serve as a reminder that healing is not only feasible but also transformative.

A Journey That Begins with Breakdown

For many, the first step toward healing doesn't look like a step forward at all. It often begins with collapse. Burnout, grief, trauma, illness these experiences can knock a person off their feet, leaving them feeling lost or broken. But this is where many healing journeys begin: in the moment when there's nothing left to pretend, nothing left to push through, and the only way forward is inward.

Take Elena, for example a corporate professional who found herself unable to get out of bed one morning after years of overwork and emotional suppression. The panic attacks had become too frequent, her sleep was non-existent, and something inside her knew she couldn't continue living that way. What followed was a journey not just of rest and medical support, but of self-reclamation. She learned to say no. She picked up painting again. She started therapy, not to "fix" herself, but to understand herself. Two years later, Elena is still on the path, but she no longer sees her breakdown as a failure it was the beginning of her return to wholeness.

The Quiet Power of Small Changes

Not every healing journey is dramatic or visible. Some unfold slowly, almost quietly. For Tariq, a former athlete dealing with chronic pain from a back injury, healing didn't come from a single surgery or breakthrough treatment. It came in the form of tiny, consistent decisions. Choosing to stretch each morning, resisting the urge to mask discomfort with alcohol, learning to listen to his body's limits instead of overriding them. Over time, he found relief not just physically, but emotionally too. His pain didn't vanish, but his relationship to it transformed.

Real healing often comes from the cumulative effect of small choices made consistently over time. These micro-decisions whether it's choosing healthier meals, committing to weekly counseling, or simply stepping outside for fresh air build momentum. They restore agency. They signal to the mind and body: You are worth caring for.

Rewriting the Narrative of Trauma

Trauma has a way of distorting time. For many survivors, years can pass while the emotional pain remains frozen in place. But healing invites movement. It invites the courage to return to the memory with new tools, new support, and a different sense of self.

Maria, a survivor of childhood abuse, began her healing journey in her mid-30s. For years, she had buried her past under layers of overachievement and perfectionism. It wasn't until she became a parent herself that the emotional weight became too heavy to carry. She entered therapy reluctantly, unsure if revisiting the past would bring healing or simply more pain. But through consistent work, trauma-informed counseling, and eventually somatic therapy, she began to feel her way through the pain rather than thinking her way around it.

Maria now speaks openly about her journey, not because the scars have disappeared, but because they no longer define her. She is living proof that trauma can be rewritten not erased, but integrated into a life that's rich with meaning and strength.

Community as Medicine

Healing is often portrayed as a solitary experience, but connection is one of its most powerful catalysts. Whether it's a circle of friends, a support group, a mentor, or a single person who listens without judgment relationships can be deeply healing.

Consider Dev, a young man recovering from opioid addiction. What saved him, he says, wasn't just rehab or detox. It was the men he met in his recovery group each carrying their own stories of pain and resilience. In their shared vulnerability, Dev found strength. In their honesty, he found hope. Community didn't solve his problems, but it reminded him that he wasn't alone. That in itself was enough to keep him moving forward.

Healing doesn't always mean becoming "independent." Sometimes, the bravest thing we can do is let ourselves be held by others, by faith, by love.

The Spiritual Dimension of Healing

For many, healing goes beyond the physical and psychological. There's a spiritual component that defies language but anchors the journey. Whether it takes the form of prayer, meditation, time in nature, or a renewed sense of purpose, spirituality can offer a sense of grounding amid uncertainty.

Arjun, who was diagnosed with a terminal illness, found peace not through curing his body, but through making peace with his life. He reconnected with his faith, forgave old grudges, and focused on the relationships that mattered most. Though his body declined, his spirit deepened. Healing, in his case, wasn't about living longer it was about living fully with the time he had left.

His narrative serves as a reminder that pain relief is not always a necessary component of recovery. Sometimes, it means learning how to hold that pain with grace, compassion, and presence.

No One-Size-Fits-All

One of the most important lessons from real-life healing journeys is that there's no universal formula. What suits one individual may not suit another. Healing might be messy or systematic, loud or quiet. It might involve therapy, medication, bodywork, journaling, creative expression, or all of the above.

But commitment is the one element that unites all of these tales. Not a commitment to perfection, but to the process. To show up for oneself, even on the hard days. Especially on the hard days.

Closing Thoughts

Real-life healing journeys don't come with neat endings or glossy finishes. They're ongoing. They unfold in layers, sometimes cycling through old wounds before revealing new growth. But they are always, at their core, acts of courage.

Each journey is a reminder that healing isn't about returning to who you were before the pain. It's about becoming someone new someone more aligned, more awake, and more whole.

These stories aren't meant to offer a step-by-step guide. They exist to remind us that healing is possible. That it takes time. And that in the quiet, uncertain spaces between breakdown and breakthrough, something sacred is always being born.

The Process of Reclaiming Memory and Self.

Reclaiming memory and self is one of the most intimate, tender, and courageous undertakings a person can embark upon. It's a process that unfolds slowly like peeling back layers of fog to reveal something that was always there, waiting. Often, it is initiated not by choice but by necessity: when the dissonance between who we are and who we've become becomes too great to ignore. In many ways, it is less about reinventing ourselves and more about remembering who we were before the world told us who to be.

This reclamation doesn't follow a linear timeline. It emerges in fragments, often triggered by subtle cues a smell, a familiar song, an old photograph, or a sudden emotional response that doesn't quite make sense on the surface. These moments, though fleeting, are doorways into something deeper. Something worth revisiting.

The Silence Before the Awakening

For many, the journey starts in silence. Not the peaceful kind, but the quiet that surrounds unspoken trauma, suppressed experiences, or forgotten truths. This silence becomes a part of everyday life, shaping decisions and self-perception without our conscious awareness. You may not even realize that you're disconnected from pieces of your story until something inside you starts asking questions that can't be ignored.

The ache to remember doesn't always feel like a longing. It might arrive as anxiety, restlessness, or a persistent sense that something just doesn't fit. This inner friction becomes the invitation to look back not for the sake of living in the past, but to understand how it shaped your present.

Memory Isn't Just a Record—It's a Living Thing

Contrary to what we're taught, memory isn't static. It's not a dusty archive stored in the back of the mind. It's alive. It breathes. It changes depending on our emotional landscape, the stories we've been told, and the healing work we've done. Reclaiming memory means being willing to question what we've accepted as truth not to rewrite history dishonestly, but to give voice to the parts of ourselves that may have been silenced, doubted, or overlooked.

In this process, clarity often comes in waves. What you remember at first may be faint or confusing. It may not make complete sense. But as you create space for these recollections to surface, patterns begin to emerge. Memories, once scattered and buried, begin to thread together like constellations, offering glimpses into a self you may have lost touch with.

The Role of the Body in Remembering

The body holds memory in ways the mind can't always articulate. A tightened jaw, a clenched fist, a sudden flutter of panic these are all forms of memory rising to the surface. Sometimes, it's not about what you remember in your head but what your body recalls without language.

This is where practices like somatic therapy, movement, breathwork, and even dance become powerful tools. They allow the body to speak its truth, often bypassing the need for intellectual understanding. Many people find that certain postures, gestures, or sensations awaken dormant memories, offering insight and emotional release that talk therapy alone may not reach.

Grieving What Was Forgotten—or Taken

One of the more difficult parts of reclaiming memory and self is grieving the time lost. Whether it's a childhood blurred by trauma, an identity suppressed to survive, or years spent living as someone you were never meant to be there is real sorrow in acknowledging what could have been.

Grieving is not about self-pity. It's about honoring your own truth. It's about saying to yourself, "You didn't deserve that," or "You did the best you could with what you had." In this space, forgiveness becomes part of healing not just for others, but for yourself.

You may find yourself mourning relationships, opportunities, or even versions of yourself you never got to be. That's okay. Healing asks us to feel, not fix.

Reclaiming Identity: Who Am I Without the Mask?

As memories surface and old wounds find language, the question inevitably arises: Who am I beneath all of this? It's both a terrifying and liberating moment. Without the roles you've played, the beliefs you've absorbed, and the coping strategies you've relied on what remains?

This is where self-reclamation moves from remembering to redefining. You start making decisions about what will remain and what will not.. You revisit dreams that were shelved. You reconnect with values that feel true, not inherited. You set boundaries that reflect your worth. Over time, your sense of self becomes less reactive and more rooted.

You might return to childhood passions. You might explore parts of yourself that never had permission to exist before your creativity, your vulnerability, your voice. This reassembly takes time, but it does occur. And each time you honor your inner truth, the distance between who you are and how you live begins to shrink.

The Importance of Safe Witnessing

Reclaiming memory and self isn't a solitary path, even if it often begins that way. Having someone bear witness to your story a therapist, a trusted friend, a mentor can be deeply healing. When someone sees your truth and doesn't look away, it affirms something sacred: you matter, and your story deserves to be heard.

Safety is crucial here. You're not obligated to tell everything to everyone. But when you find the right spaces, sharing can become a powerful form of integration. It reminds you that you don't have to carry your history in silence anymore.

Integration Over Perfection

One of the most common misconceptions about healing is that there's a finish line a moment where everything clicks into place, and the past no longer affects you. In truth, healing is more about integration than resolution.

You don't forget. You don't erase. You carry your memories with wisdom, not weight. You understand your triggers, not because you've eliminated them, but because you've befriended them. You learn how to care for the younger versions of yourself that still live inside you. And in doing so, you become more whole.

A Personal Reclamation

Reclaiming memory and self is deeply personal. No two journeys look the same. For some, it involves confronting trauma. For others, it's about rediscovering joy. It might include reconnecting with cultural heritage, healing from systemic harm, or simply learning how to speak to yourself with more kindness.

Whatever shape it takes, the process is brave. It asks you to sit with discomfort. To risk feeling more before you feel better. But it also gives something irreplaceable in return: a self that feels fully inhabited, a life that feels authentically yours.

Lessons Learned from Clients

In the field of healing whether through psychotherapy, coaching, bodywork, or holistic wellness practitioners are often seen as the guides, the ones who carry tools, offer insight, and provide support. But those who spend years walking alongside others in their healing journeys quickly realize something else: the clients are teachers, too. In every shared silence, breakthrough, setback, or revelation, there are lessons profound ones that shape not just how we practice, but how we live, relate, and understand what it means to be human.

Training sessions and textbooks don't contain these lessons. They come from real people navigating real pain, resilience, confusion, hope, and transformation. They come from the quiet moments of honesty, the unfiltered stories, and the courage it takes for someone to show up week after week and do the work of facing themselves.

1. Healing Is Not Linear

One of the most consistent lessons clients have taught is that healing rarely unfolds in straight lines. The reality is much more complicated, despite our yearning for clean schedules and progressions.People may take two steps forward and then one or sometimes three steps back. That doesn't mean failure. It means they're human.

Sam, a client dealing with grief after the sudden loss of his brother, once said, "I thought I was done crying, but today it hit me like it just happened." That statement held so much truth. Healing often revisits us in waves. Clients like Sam remind us that progress can include revisiting pain not to regress, but to deepen the healing each time.

As practitioners, learning to honor each person's unique rhythm is essential. Clients teach us to be patient, flexible, and open to the unexpected. They show us that detours are not dead ends, and that every part of the journey has value.

2. People Are Incredibly Resilient—Even When They Don't See It

There is something awe-inspiring about witnessing someone face their deepest fears, losses, or traumas and still find a way to continue. Many clients don't recognize their own resilience, especially when they feel broken or overwhelmed. But the very act of seeking support is a testament to their inner strength.

Lina, a young woman recovering from complex childhood abuse, once shared, "Sometimes I think I'm weak for needing therapy." But the truth was just the opposite. Her ability to ask for help, to sit with unbearable emotions, to question long-held beliefs about herself that was strength in its purest form.

Clients teach us that resilience doesn't always look like bold declarations or big life changes. Sometimes it looks like simply showing up. Choosing to stay. Continuing the conversation even when it's hard. That kind of quiet courage is deeply humbling to witness.

3. Authentic Connection Heals

Over the years, it becomes clear that one of the most transformative aspects of any therapeutic process isn't just the techniques or interventions it's the relationship itself. Clients often enter spaces with walls built high from past betrayals, neglect, or emotional starvation. But something shifts when they realize that this space is different. That here, they are seen. Heard. Not judged.

It's often in those moments of genuine connection when a therapist says, "That sounds really painful, and I'm here with you," or when a client risks telling the truth for the first time that healing begins to take root.

Clients like Jordan, who initially spoke in clinical, detached language about their experiences, eventually softened not because of pressure, but because they felt safe enough to be real. That shift wasn't forced; it was earned, and it was sacred.

From clients, we learn that the human need to be witnessed and accepted is not optional it's essential. And when that need is met in a respectful, attuned way, transformation becomes possible.

4. Listening Is an Act of Love

Hearing and listening are two very different things. Clients teach this lesson again and again Sometimes, what someone needs most isn't a solution, a diagnosis, or advice it's presence. Attuned, undivided presence.

Clients often carry stories they've never told another soul. When they share those stories and are met with steady, non-reactive attention, it can shift something fundamental. It says, "You matter. Your story matters." That simple acknowledgment can be more healing than any intervention.

In the words of Rashid, a man processing racial trauma and identity struggles, "You didn't interrupt. You didn't try to fix it. You just sat with me in it. That's what I needed." That moment became a powerful reminder that silence, when grounded in care, can speak volumes.

5. Labels Never Tell the Whole Story

Working with clients over time often reveals the limits of diagnostic categories. Labels can offer clarity and a framework, yes but they can never encapsulate the entirety of a person. A diagnosis might describe what's happening, but it doesn't define who someone is.

Emily was labeled with borderline personality disorder, a term that carried stigma and a sense of hopelessness. But beneath that label was a woman who had endured unspeakable loss, who craved connection, and who had developed fierce survival strategies. She couldn't be reduced to a diagnosis as her story developed.

Clients teach us to see beyond the label to meet the human being underneath. They remind us to hold both complexity and compassion, to work with the whole person rather than reducing them to symptoms or pathology.

6. Humor and Lightness Have Their Place

Amidst all the heaviness that can come with emotional work, clients often surprise us with laughter, irony, or moments of levity. Humor, even in dark times, becomes a form of resistance a way of reclaiming power and remembering joy.

Some of the most meaningful sessions have included both tears and laughter. Clients remind us that healing doesn't have to be solemn all the time. Lightness can coexist with pain. It doesn't diminish the seriousness of the work it makes it more human.

7. Each Story Changes You

Perhaps the most profound lesson is this: you don't leave this work unchanged. Each client leaves an imprint. Every story heard, every breakthrough witnessed, every struggle held shapes you.

There's a kind of mutuality in the therapeutic relationship. While clients are changed by the space you hold, you are changed by their courage, honesty, and presence. It's not about becoming entangled in their pain, but about being affected in a way that deepens your humanity.

From Maya, who taught me what grace under pressure looks like, to Leo, who redefined what vulnerability can be each person becomes a silent teacher. And for that, practitioners remain forever students.

Final Thoughts

The lessons learned from clients cannot be measured by credentials or years of experience alone. They live in the quiet moments, the shared breath, the unspoken trust that builds over time. These lessons don't just inform the work they transform it. They humble you, stretch you, and remind you why you chose this path in the first place.

In the end, healing is not something done to someone it's something done with them. And those we walk with often end up guiding us just as much as we guide them.

CHAPTER EIGHT

Tools for Self-Exploration

Journaling as a Healing Tool

The act of writing anything down has a tremendous amount of power. In a world that rarely slows down, journaling offers a quiet space to pause, reflect, and breathe. It's more than just a notebook and ink it's a sanctuary for your thoughts, a canvas for your emotions, and, in many cases, a tool for genuine healing.

At its core, journaling is simple. You write. But what unfolds in that simplicity can be transformative. Whether it's processing grief, managing anxiety, healing from trauma, or simply navigating the ups and downs of life, journaling can help you better understand yourself and your experiences.

What makes journaling so unique is that it's deeply personal. There are no rules. You can scribble, ramble, write in full sentences or fragments. You can be angry, joyful, confused, or heartbroken. The page doesn't judge. It doesn't interrupt. It listens. And in that silent witnessing, healing begins.

Many therapists recommend journaling because it externalizes thoughts that otherwise loop endlessly in the mind. When we're overwhelmed, our brains tend to swirl with feelings, fears, and fragmented memories. Writing them down allows us to release some of that mental pressure. It's like unpacking a heavy bag you might not throw everything away, but even laying it all out helps you see what you're carrying and why.

The ability of journaling to reveal patterns is among its most important features. When you write regularly, you start to notice recurring emotions, themes, and triggers. This self-awareness can be incredibly empowering. It enables you to react more thoughtfully.Furthermore, the first significant step in the healing process is frequently consciousness.

Journaling can also offer closure. We don't always have the opportunity to express what we need to.Whether it's to a loved one who's passed, a friendship that ended badly, or a chapter of life that closed too soon, writing can serve as a form of emotional completion. You can write letters you'll never send, have conversations you never got to finish, or simply say goodbye in your own way.

Another beautiful thing about journaling is that it creates a tangible record of growth. Looking back at past entries can be humbling, even emotional. You can see where you've been how far you've come, the storms you survived, the strength you didn't know you had. That kind of perspective can be deeply healing, especially during tough times when progress feels invisible.

Of course, like any tool, journaling works best when it's used intentionally. It's not about forcing yourself to write daily or turning your entries into polished essays. It's about being honest. Being real.as well as allowing oneself to feel without any filters.

There are many different ways to journal, depending on what you need. Some people use prompts questions that spark reflection.Others like writing in a free-flowing, stream-of-consciousness style.Some keep gratitude journals, focusing on the positive. Others write to process pain or trauma. There's no one-size-fits-all approach. The beauty lies in its flexibility.

For those dealing with mental health challenges, journaling can be a grounding practice. It helps organize thoughts, track emotional patterns, and give shape to the chaos that often accompanies anxiety or depression. Combined with professional support, it can be a deeply effective tool in the healing journey.It can be a very powerful aid in the healing process when used in conjunction with expert assistance.

Even in moments of joy, journaling serves as a kind of emotional anchor. It helps you savor experiences, capture meaningful memories, and cultivate a deeper appreciation for life. And when hard times hit, those joyful entries can be a powerful reminder of better days and the possibility of better days ahead.

Ultimately, journaling is a quiet rebellion in a noisy world. It asks you to slow down. To look inward. To listen to yourself in a way that few people ever do. And in that listening, healing takes root not always fast or dramatic, but real, steady, and lasting.

So if you're holding onto something heavy, or just need a safe space to land, pick up a pen. Start where you are. No pressure. No perfection. Just your truth, written one word at a time.

Art and Creative Expression in Processing Trauma

Trauma, in its many forms, often carves silence into the human experience silence in words, in emotions, and in understanding. For many, the path to healing isn't paved with language, logic, or straightforward conversation. Instead, it winds through color, shape, rhythm, and story. This is where art steps in not simply as a pastime or aesthetic indulgence, but as a powerful, transformative tool that helps people process and make sense of pain that often defies explanation.

When traditional talk therapy feels too direct or overwhelming, creative expression offers an alternative door to the inner self. Artistic processes whether painting, drawing, sculpting, writing, dancing, or making music allow people to express what they might not yet be able to say. It's a way of externalizing what's been buried deep inside, giving shape to the intangible, and often, unnameable emotions tied to trauma. A person might not have words for their sorrow or fear, but they might paint a chaotic swirl of dark tones, or write a poem that flickers with subtle metaphors. Through creation, they begin to feel seen even by themselves.

Art doesn't demand perfection. It doesn't judge. This unconditional freedom is critical for trauma survivors, whose experiences may have left them feeling powerless or shamed. The very act of creating something something wholly their own can be an act of reclamation. It restores a sense of agency. What was once a feeling of being undone can begin to reassemble itself in a mosaic of expression.

What's particularly special about creative expression in the context of trauma is its ability to bypass the rational mind. Trauma isn't just stored in memories; it resides in the body, in the nervous system. Traditional therapies may struggle to reach these embodied scars. But dance, for example, allows a person to move through emotion physically. Music can resonate with emotional states that words can't touch. Writing, especially in stream-of-consciousness or narrative form, can help organize a chaotic inner world, giving structure to fragmented memories and feelings.

The act of creating art is frequently more significant than the finished piece. A painting doesn't need to be technically impressive to be meaningful. A song doesn't need to be in tune. What the act of creation reveals is what gives it value. It invites the person into a flow state a mindful, present-focused zone where healing can begin. This presence is particularly important, because trauma often fragments time, trapping people in a loop of past events. Art brings people back to the now.

Another profound aspect of creative expression is its capacity to connect people. whether it is through internet platforms, community murals, open mics, or group workshops. It serves as a reminder that although sorrow is extremely personal, it is not a lonely experience. Others have walked similar paths. Others have found beauty in their brokenness too.

Over time, creative practices can become rituals of resilience. A trauma survivor who writes a daily journal entry, sketches their emotions, or strums a guitar string when feeling overwhelmed, is engaging in acts of self-soothing and self-validation. These small, personal rituals create a rhythm of care and reflection. They say, "I am still here. I am still creating."

Of course, creative expression is not a one-size-fits-all cure. Not every survivor will find solace in the arts, and that's okay. But for many, it opens a door that was previously locked or invisible altogether. In the hands of a compassionate therapist, art can become a tool for dialogue and discovery. In the quiet of one's own room, it can be a sacred space for truth-telling and transformation.

Ultimately, the role of art in processing trauma lies in its humanity. It honors the complexity of pain, the resilience of spirit, and the infinite ways we make meaning from suffering. Through brushstrokes, melodies, words, and movement, we begin to stitch ourselves back together not perfectly, but beautifully, and in our own time.

In the noise of everyday life, our connection to our bodies often becomes distant or neglected. We go through motions, carry stress, and sometimes lose track of what our bodies are telling us. Guided exercises for body awareness are designed to gently bring attention back to our physical selves not just as vessels, but as living, breathing systems full of sensation, emotion, and subtle cues. These practices promote mindfulness, reduce stress, and foster a deeper understanding of how we move, feel, and exist in our bodies.

The Foundations of Body Awareness

Before diving into the exercises, it helps to understand what body awareness actually means. It's more than simply knowing you have hands and feet it's about sensing them in space, recognizing how they move, and being attuned to how they feel in different states. It involves proprioception (the sense of where your body is in space) and interoception (the ability to feel internal body signals like hunger, heartbeat, or breathing).

Developing this awareness can improve posture, coordination, emotional regulation, and overall wellbeing. It's a key component in practices like yoga, somatic therapy, martial arts, and dance.

Exercise 1: The Full-Body Scan

The body scan is a classic mindfulness practice that encourages you to systematically tune into different areas of your body. It's often done lying down, but it can also be practiced seated.

How to Do It:

1. If it feels secure, locate a peaceful, comfortable area and close your eyes.

2. Begin by noticing your breath without changing it.

3. Go to the top of your head and focus. Notice any sensations temperature, tingling, pressure.

4. Slowly move your attention downward: face, neck, shoulders, arms, hands, chest, belly, hips, legs, and feet.

5. Pause at each area for a few breaths, simply noticing what's there without judgment.

6. Bring your thoughts back gently if they stray. This exercise helps build an intimate understanding of your physical state and can uncover areas of tension you weren't even aware of.

Exercise 2: Breath and Movement Synchronization.

Pairing breath with simple movements can deepen the mind-body connection and center your awareness.

How to Do It:

1. When sitting or standing comfortably, keep your spine straight.

2. Inhale and raise your arms slowly overhead.

3. Exhale and lower them back down.

4. Continue doing this slowly and deliberately for a few breaths.

5. 5. Take particular note of the contraction and relaxation of the muscles.

As you move, try to remain aware of every sensation muscle contractions, air moving through your nose, the rhythm of your breathing. It's not about perfection; it's about presence.

Exercise 3: Mirror Work

Using a mirror can create a powerful sense of embodiment, especially when exploring posture and alignment.

How to Do It:

1. Stand in front of a full-length mirror.

2. Start by observing your natural posture without making any adjustments.

3. Adjust your posture gradually by elongating your spine, rolling your shoulders back, and aligning your feet.

4. Notice how these changes feel. Is there strain? Relief?

5. Practice different movements reaching, squatting, stretching and observe the way your body engages.

This is an excellent method for recognizing repetitive positions and promoting a more neutral, helpful posture.

Exercise 4: Sensory Awareness Walk

Take a slow walk, indoors or outside, but with the intent to deeply notice the sensory experience of moving.

How to Do It:

1. Begin walking slowly, without rushing.

2. Observe the way your feet touch the floor.

3. Observe how the weight changes from one side to the other.

4. Tune into what you feel in your legs, hips, spine, arms, and even fingers.

5. Add layers—what do you hear? Smell? See?

This type of walk is less about destination and more about discovery. One step at a time, it's a moving meditation.

Exercise 5: Emotional Body Mapping

Our emotions often show up in the body before we consciously realize what we're feeling. This exercise helps connect emotional states to physical sensations.

How to Do It:

1. Sit quietly and think of a recent emotion joy, frustration, sadness.

2. In what part of my body do I feel this?

3. Place your attention on that area. Is it warm? Tight? Heavy? Light?

4. Let the sensation unfold without trying to change it.

5. You can even draw an outline of your body on paper and color in where you feel things, if it helps to visualize.

This practice builds emotional intelligence and allows you to catch patterns over time.

Exercise 6: Tension and Release

Conscious tension and release help build awareness by exaggerating the contrast between tightness and ease.

How to Do It:

1. Start with your hands clench them tightly for five seconds.

2. Then release and observe the difference.

3. Move through the body arms, shoulders, face, legs, and feet using the same pattern.

4. After each release, pause and feel the relaxation spreading.

Over time, this helps train the nervous system to recognize tension earlier and release it more easily.

Integrating Body Awareness into Daily Life

These exercises are tools not one-time events. The real magic happens when body awareness becomes a habit. You can practice during daily routines:

While brushing your teeth, pay attention to the feelings in your body.

Checking in with your posture while sitting at your desk.

focusing on your breathing before taking a call

It doesn't take hours of practice or expensive equipment to develop body awareness. It just asks for attention, patience, and presence.

Guided Exercises for Body Awareness

Body awareness is more than just knowing you have a body it's about understanding how it moves, feels, and interacts with the space around you. Developing this sense can enhance coordination, reduce stress, prevent injuries, and promote a stronger connection between the mind and body. Through guided exercises, anyonenfrom athletes to everyday folks can tune into their bodies more deeply. Let's explore how.

1. Grounding Through Breath and Stillness

The breath is the starting point for bodily awareness.Locate a peaceful area where you can comfortably sit or lie down.Shut your eyes and inhale deeply through your nose, allowing your stomach to rise.Slowly exhale through your mouth. Repeat this cycle several times, letting each breath slow your thoughts and calm your nervous system.

Pay attention to the connection between your body and the earth as you breathe. You should feel your back in alignment, your legs supported, and your feet planted.This simple grounding technique helps you come back to the present moment and opens the door to deeper bodily awareness.

2. **Body Scan Meditation**

A body scan is a step-by-step journey through your physical self. Start at your toes. Notice any sensations warmth, coolness, tingling, or even numbness.Just observe without passing judgment or attempting to alter anything.

Slowly work your way up: ankles, calves, knees, thighs. Take a moment to observe the sensations in each area.Are there areas of tightness or fatigue? Does any part feel light, heavy, or completely neutral? Continue up through your torso, hands, arms, neck, and finally your face. A strong sense of inner listening is fostered by this practice.

3. **Movement Exploration**

Once you've built awareness through stillness, incorporate gentle movement. Begin with simple stretches raise your arms, roll your shoulders, rotate your neck. Notice how each motion feels. Is there resistance or ease? Move slowly enough that your attention stays with the movement, rather than the destination.

You might try intuitive movement: let your body guide you. Change your weight from one foot to the other, twist, reach, or sway from side to side. There's no right or wrong. This type of exploration invites creativity while strengthening the brain-body connection.

4. **Mirror Work and Alignment Practice**

Examine your posture while standing in front of a mirror. Are your shoulders even? Is your head aligned with your spine? Are your knees locked or relaxed? Use the reflection not to critique, but to learn. Make small adjustments and notice how they change your balance or breathing.

Practicing alignment increases physical awareness and helps prevent long-term strain. Over time, you'll start recognizing poor posture or imbalance throughout your day and instinctively correct it.

5. **Walking Meditation**

This isn't about getting from point A to B it's about noticing every step. Locate a peaceful area where you can stroll unhindered and slowly. As you move, feel your heel touch down, your foot roll, your toes lift off. Breathe in time with your steps and allow your arms to swing freely.

This deliberate form of walking draws your attention to balance, coordination, and rhythm. It's particularly useful for calming an anxious mind or for breaking up long periods of sitting.

6. Engaging the Senses

Body awareness isn't limited to muscles and bones. It also involves tuning into your sensory world. Shut your eyes and hear what you hear. What is the sensation of your clothes on your skin? Can you taste the air, feel its temperature?

You can also use props: roll a textured ball under your foot or gently massage your arms with different fabrics. Noticing how your body responds to different sensations helps sharpen your nervous system's sensitivity and responsiveness.

7. Progressive Muscle Release

Each muscle group is purposefully tensed and then relaxed during this workout.Begin with your feet: scrunch your toes tightly, hold for a few seconds, and release. Move up the body in sections calves, thighs, abdomen, chest, hands, arms, shoulders, face tightening and relaxing as you go.

You can better discern between stress and relaxation with this technique. Over time, you'll be able to recognize when you're holding stress in a certain area and consciously let it go.

8. Journaling Your Experience

After every session, spend a few minutes noting your observations.Did a particular stretch feel easier today? Was there a part of your body that spoke louder than the rest? Were there emotions tied to certain sensations?

Reflective writing adds another layer of mindfulness to the process. It also helps track changes over time and deepens your understanding of how your body responds to stress, movement, and care.

Final Thoughts

Guided body awareness exercises are a gentle yet powerful way to reconnect with yourself. They teach patience, foster resilience, and promote well-being from the inside out. The advantages mount regardless of how long you practice five minutes a day or longer sessions. You become not only more in tune with your physical self but also more grounded, calm, and confident in your everyday life.

CHAPTER NINE

Building a Support System

Finding the Right Professionals

The best results often come from good communication and mutual understanding, not just skill.

It's also worth noting that the "right" professional for you might not be the most expensive, the most decorated, or even the most experienced. Chemistry matters. Someone who truly listens, understands your goals, and is willing to collaborate can be far more valuable than a high-profile expert who doesn't quite get your vision.

Don't rush the process. It can be tempting to jump in with the first person who seems like a fit, especially when you're excited to get started. But investing a little extra time in the beginning to ensure you're working with the right people can save you time, money, and stress down the line.

Also, trust your instincts. If something feels off during early conversations maybe the communication is unclear, or the energy isn't right it's okay to move on. A working relationship built on trust, respect, and open dialogue is essential for success.

Finally, remember that finding the right professionals is a two-way street. They are assessing you in the same way that you are assessing them. Clearly state your goals, spending limit, and deadlines. Be honest about your needs and where you might need extra guidance. A good professional will appreciate transparency and be better equipped to serve you when they have a clear understanding of the big picture.

In the end, finding the right professionals isn't just about credentials it's about connection. You'll know when it's the proper fit. Things will click. Conversations will flow. Progress will feel natural. And most importantly, you'll be one step closer to turning your vision into reality with a trusted partner by your side.

Community and Connection: The Threads That Hold Us Together

In a world that often emphasizes individualism and personal success, it's easy to overlook the quiet, powerful force of community. Yet, it's within communities whether formed by family, friends, neighborhoods, or shared interests that we find our most enduring sense of belonging. At its heart, community is not just a group of people living near each other. It's the emotional, psychological, and often spiritual web that ties people together in shared experience, mutual support, and a common purpose.

Conversely, connection is the unseen thread that binds a group together. It's when you meet someone and you understand them right away. It's the comfort of being seen, heard, and valued just as you are. Connection is what turns a collection of strangers into a support system, a team, or even a family.

The Need for Belonging

Human beings are wired for connection. From our earliest days, we rely on others not just for survival, but for identity. Who we are is shaped in part by the people around us. We laugh more when we're with friends. We grieve better when we're not alone. We heal faster, grow stronger, and become more resilient when we're part of a community that cares.

Think about how different life feels when you have someone to call when good news comes or when things fall apart. That instinct to share, to reach out, to include others in our stories is not weakness; it's deeply human.

Communities Come in Many Forms

Not all communities look the same. Some are built around physical proximity a neighborhood, a school, a workplace. Others form through shared interests or values, like book clubs, spiritual groups, online forums, or volunteer organizations. What matters most isn't the structure, but the feeling. Do you feel safe? Accepted? Understood?

Even fleeting communities a support group you attend for a few weeks, a team you join for a short season can leave a lasting impact. They serve as a reminder that life is not meant to be lived alone. They challenge the myth of self-sufficiency by offering help, perspective, and a sense of shared humanity.

Connection Requires Effort

While community is a beautiful idea, it doesn't happen by accident. It requires intention. You have to show up. You have to be willing to listen, to share, to offer help even when it's inconvenient. And sometimes, you have to repair the fabric of community when it tears through forgiveness, understanding, and open dialogue.

Connection also means being vulnerable. It's one thing to be around people; it's another to let them really see you.That type of honesty fosters trust, and trust is the foundation of any lasting relationship.

The Digital Age: A Double-Edged Sword

Technology has redefined what it means to connect. Social media platforms allow us to keep in touch with people across the globe, but they can also create a false sense of closeness. A "like" is not the same as a conversation. A comment thread doesn't always replace a heart-to-heart. That's not to say digital communities aren't real they absolutely can be but they require the same care and authenticity as in-person relationships.

Sometimes, the challenge is to disconnect from the noise in order to truly connect with the people in front of us. Real presence, undistracted and engaged, is increasingly rare and increasingly valuable.

The Power of Shared Experience

One of the most profound ways we bond with others is through shared experiences. These don't have to be monumental. They can be as simple as cooking a meal together, playing music, or facing a challenge side-by-side. When we go through something together especially something hard it creates a bond that words alone can't form.

Communities built through shared struggles are often the most enduring. Survivors of illness, activists fighting for change, students navigating the same tough classes these are connections forged in fire. They teach us empathy, compassion, and the strength that comes from standing together.

Giving Back: The Heart of Community

Being part of a community isn't just about what you get it's also about what you give. Acts of kindness, small or large, ripple through a community in ways we don't always see. Offering help without expecting anything in return, checking in on someone just because, making space for others to speak these gestures build the kind of community we all want to be part of.

And it works both ways. Giving fosters gratitude. Gratitude deepens connection. And deep connections, in turn, create the kind of communities that can weather storms and celebrate joy with equal sincerity.

In Conclusion

Community and connection are not luxuries. They're essential to a full, meaningful life. They serve as a reminder that we belong to something greater than ourselves. They root us, even in uncertain times. And perhaps most importantly, they help us remember that we are never truly alone.

So, in a fast-paced world that often pulls us apart, may we take time to lean in to reach out, to listen more, to build bridges instead of walls. Because in the end, it's our connections with others that give life its richest meaning.

1. **Therapy and Counseling**

Professional therapy remains one of the most effective ways to process pain and gain clarity. Depending on your needs, you might consider:

Individual Therapy – One-on-one sessions with a licensed counselor can offer personalized support and help you navigate complex feelings.

Group Therapy – Sharing your journey with others who understand can reduce isolation and foster a sense of belonging.

Trauma-Informed Therapy – For those recovering from specific traumatic experiences, working with a trauma-informed therapist can be especially healing.

When seeking a therapist, look for someone who aligns with your values and communicates in a way that makes you feel seen and safe.

2. **Support Groups**

Healing often requires connection. Support groups offer a forum for talking, listening, and connecting. Whether you're dealing with anxiety, loss, addiction, or abuse recovery, there's likely a group that fits your needs.

Organizations like NAMI (National Alliance on Mental Illness), Alcoholics Anonymous, and GriefShare offer both in-person and virtual communities. These spaces remind you that you're not walking the path alone.

3. **Books and Literature**

Books can be powerful companions on your healing journey. From memoirs to self-help guides, the right words can speak directly to your soul. Some titles may provide coping strategies, while others offer reassurance and understanding. Look for works written by mental health professionals, survivors, or spiritual leaders who have walked similar roads.

Libraries, independent bookstores, and online platforms often have curated lists of titles that focus on mental wellness and personal growth.

4. **Mind-Body Practices**

Healing happens in the body as much as in the mind. Activities that integrate physical movement with mindfulness can be incredibly restorative. Consider exploring:

Yoga – Especially trauma-sensitive or restorative yoga, which focuses on gentle movement and awareness.

Meditation and Breathwork – These practices help regulate your nervous system and foster inner peace.

Tai Chi or Qi Gong – Gentle, flowing movements that encourage harmony and grounding.

Many communities offer donation-based classes or free online sessions to make these practices accessible.

5. Creative Outlets

Art can convey ideas that words can't always.Painting, writing, dancing, or performing music are all forms of creative expression that can be therapeutic.Being able to freely communicate your own feelings is more important than being an expert. Art therapy is also a structured option for those looking to explore healing through guided creativity, often under the support of a trained professional.

6. **Spiritual and Faith-Based Resources**

For many, healing is deeply tied to faith or spirituality. Whether you follow a specific religion or identify with a more general sense of spirituality, connecting with a community or spiritual leader can bring comfort.

Meditation retreats, prayer circles, sacred texts, and interfaith groups can offer insights, support, and a sense of higher purpose. Trust in what resonates with your spirit.

7. **Digital Tools and Mobile Apps**

In today's world, technology offers healing support at your fingertips. Apps like Calm, Insight Timer, Headspace, or BetterHelp provide guided meditations, therapy access, journaling tools, and more. These platforms can offer daily encouragement and be especially useful between therapy sessions or when support feels distant.

8. Holistic Health Services

Sometimes, healing benefits from an integrative approach. Acupuncture, massage therapy, herbal medicine, and nutritional counseling can complement emotional and mental recovery. These methods help the body release stress, balance energy, and support physical wellness as part of the bigger healing picture.

Before exploring alternative methods, it's a good idea to consult your healthcare provider to ensure safety and compatibility with your current treatments.

9. Safe Spaces and Sanctuary

Sometimes healing just requires a place to breathe. A quiet room. A nature trail. A meditation cushion. Creating or finding physical spaces that bring you peace whether in your home or community can be transformative. These sanctuaries, no matter how simple, provide a refuge from chaos and a chance to reconnect with yourself.

10. Trusted Relationships

Never underestimate the power of a caring friend or loved one. Healing thrives in environments of empathy and understanding. Be in the company of individuals who will listen to you without passing judgment, who will affirm your experience, and who will support you even if you remain silent.

If those relationships are hard to find, don't give up. Sometimes, chosen family or online communities can become your circle of strength.

Final Thoughts

There's no one-size-fits-all map for healing. What suits one individual could not suit another. The key is staying curious, open, and compassionate toward yourself as you explore what helps you heal.

You are allowed to take your time. You are allowed to feel everything. And you are absolutely worthy of healing again and again.

CONCLUSION

Reflections on the Journey of Healing.

The route to healing is not a straight one; rather, it is a meandering one that passes through woods, up rocky slopes, and across vast spaces. There are moments where you feel as though you've survived and that the worst is over. Then there are days when you're brought to your knees by a memory, a setback, or a wave of emotion you thought you'd already dealt with. What I've come to understand is that healing isn't about reaching some perfect, untouched version of yourself it's about becoming whole again, not in spite of what hurt you, but alongside it.

For anyone who's walked this road, you know it doesn't begin with a lightning bolt or a dramatic revelation. More often, it begins quietly with a whisper that something needs to change. Maybe it's exhaustion.

Maybe it's the realization that you can't keep going the way you've been. The first step toward recovery is frequently the most frightening, regardless of the trigger.Admitting that something is broken requires bravery.

Healing asks you to slow down as you proceed.We live in a world that idolizes speed and productivity, but emotional recovery doesn't fit into that mold. It's not efficient. It doesn't run on schedules. It requires space space to feel, to fall apart, and to put yourself back together in a new way. And sometimes, the hardest part is simply giving yourself permission to feel what you feel without judgment.

One of the most transformative parts of the healing journey, for me, was learning how to sit with pain without rushing to fix it. I had believed that healing entailed totally removing the hurt.But over time, I realized that it's more about changing your relationship with the pain. It's about acknowledging it, learning from it, and slowly, gently letting it become part of your story not the whole story, but a chapter in it.

The people we meet along the way can also shape our healing. Some arrive like anchors, grounding us when everything feels unstable. Others may walk away, unable to hold space for the version of us that's breaking and rebuilding. And that, too, is part of the process learning who can stay in your life as you grow, and letting go of what no longer supports your well-being.

Grief and healing often go hand in hand. Whether you're healing from a loss, a betrayal, trauma, or a season of self-neglect, you have to mourn what once was. There's an ache for the innocence you lost, the time you can't get back, or the version of yourself that was deeply wounded. Honoring that grief, rather than running from it, is essential.We create space for fresh starts while we are grieving.

And somewhere along the way usually when you least expect it you start to notice change. Maybe it's the first deep breath that doesn't carry the weight of sadness.

Maybe it's a laugh that catches you off guard. Or maybe it's the quiet sense of peace that sneaks in during an ordinary moment. These are the subtle signs that healing is happening. Not loudly. Not all at once. But steadily.

Healing also teaches you boundaries the importance of saying no, of protecting your energy, of recognizing what environments nurture your growth and which ones deplete it.Keeping your peace is not selfish; it is essential.And once you've done the work to reclaim your sense of self, you become less willing to let anything compromise it.

One of the unexpected gifts of healing is empathy. Once you've walked through fire, you recognize the smoke in someone else's eyes. You become softer, more compassionate not just toward others, but toward yourself. You begin to understand that everyone carries invisible wounds, and that kindness can be a lifeline.

In hindsight, I believe that healing is a continuous process.It's not a box to check or a milestone to conquer.It's an ongoing process of self-discovery that lasts a lifetime.And the beauty of it is that, even in the midst of pain, we discover resilience we didn't know we had. We uncover strength in our vulnerability, wisdom in our scars, and hope in the darkest places.

So if you're in the thick of it hurting, questioning, holding on by a thread know this: it won't always feel this heavy. You are not alone. And there is a version of you, not so far from now, who will look back with pride at how far you've come. Keep going. The road may be long, but there is light ahead.

The Future of Mind-Body Practices

In a world that's constantly buzzing with distractions, the mind-body connection is becoming more than a wellness trend it's evolving into a fundamental part of how we live, heal, and thrive. From ancient practices like yoga and Tai Chi to emerging technologies like neurofeedback and biohacking, mind-body practices are rapidly transforming.Looking ahead, it is evident that these approaches are about to undergo a significant change that will combine the knowledge of the past with the creativity of the future.

A Shift in Global Consciousness

One of the most powerful forces shaping the future of mind-body practices is a growing global awareness of holistic well-being. People are increasingly recognizing that physical health isn't just about what we eat or how often we exercise. Mental and emotional well-being are gaining equal weight. Stress-related illnesses, burnout, and anxiety have sparked a worldwide search for deeper healing methods. As this consciousness evolves, so does the demand for practices that engage both the mind and the body in harmony.

These days, the popularity of yoga studios, breathwork sessions, and meditation applications is more than just a wellness trend. These tools are becoming integral to daily routines across all walks of life from corporate professionals to school children. The future lies in deeper integration of these practices into mainstream systems like healthcare, education, and even urban planning.

Blending Ancient Wisdom with Modern Science

Ancient traditions hold valuable insights into the mind-body relationship. Practices such as mindfulness, qigong, and Ayurveda have stood the test of time because they address the individual as a whole. What's exciting now is how modern science is validating and expanding on those traditions.

For instance, neuroimaging has allowed researchers to observe the brain's response to meditation in real-time. Regular mindfulness practice has been shown to alter the structure of the brain, especially in regions linked to attention, empathy, and emotional control. These findings are not only fascinating they're encouraging the medical community to take mind-body interventions more seriously.

As research continues to back these approaches, we're likely to see more collaboration between healthcare professionals and holistic practitioners. Prescription pads may soon include mindfulness training or yoga therapy alongside traditional treatments.

The Role of Technology

Technology, once considered a barrier to mindfulness, is now emerging as a bridge. Devices like wearable EEG headbands, heart rate monitors, and AI-driven meditation apps are making it easier than ever to track, personalize, and deepen mind-body practices. Virtual reality (VR) is being used to create immersive meditative environments, helping people escape from stressful settings and reconnect with calm, even if only for a few minutes.

Biofeedback, once restricted to clinical settings, is becoming accessible to the average person. These tools empower users to observe how thoughts and emotions influence their physiology, fostering a deeper understanding of their mind-body link.

But as we rely more on technology, there's also a growing movement to maintain the soul of these practices. Many thought leaders emphasize that while gadgets can guide us, true transformation still comes from presence, discipline, and intention. The challenge for the future will be to use technology as an aid, not a crutch.

Personalized, Inclusive, and Culturally Sensitive Practices

A Return to Stillness

Ironically, as the pace of life accelerates, we may find ourselves circling back to something very simple: stillness. The future of mind-body practices doesn't necessarily mean more complexity. In many ways, it's a return to presence, a re-learning of how to be with ourselves in silence and without judgment.

This resurgence of stillness is perhaps the most revolutionary act in our attention-fractured culture. It's a quiet rebellion against noise, an invitation to inhabit our lives more fully, and a testament to the enduring power of being deeply connected to the body, the breath, and the present moment.

Final Thoughts

The future of mind-body practices is not about abandoning the old or blindly chasing the new. It's about integration bridging ancient wisdom with cutting-edge science, technology with tradition, and inner work with outer change. As this field continues to grow, it invites each of us to participate in a more conscious, connected, and compassionate way of living. Not just for our own healing, but for the collective well-being of our communities and the planet.

Printed in Dunstable, United Kingdom